SOCIOLOGY IN FOCUS SERIES
General Editor: Murray Morison

Race and Ethnicity

Mike O'Donnell
Senior Lecturer in Education and Sociology,
Bath College of Higher Education

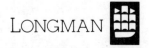

LONGMAN

LONGMAN GROUP UK LIMITED
Longman House, Burnt Mill, Harlow, Essex CM20 2JE, UK and Associated Companies throughout the World.

Published in the United States of America by Longman Inc., New York.

© **Longman Group UK Limited 1991**
All rights reserved; no part of this publication may be reproduced, stored in a retrieval system, or transmitted in any form or by any means, electronic, mechanical, photocopying, recording, or otherwise, without the prior written permission of the Publishers.

First published 1991
ISBN 0 582 03896 0

Set in 10/11pt Bembo, Linotron 202

Produced by Longman Malaysia Sdn. Bhd.
Printed in Malaysia by Percetakan Anda Sdn. Bhd.,
Sri Petaling, Kuala Lumpur

British Library Cataloguing in Publication Data
O'Donnell, Mike
  Race and ethnicity. – (Sociology in focus series)
  1. Race relations   2. Great Britain
  I. Title   II. Series
  305.800941

  ISBN 0-582-03896-0

Library of Congress Cataloging-in-Publication Data
O'Donnell, Mike.
  Race and ethnicity/Mike O'Donnell.
    p.   cm. – (Sociology in focus series)
  Includes bibliographical references and index.
  ISBN 0-582-03896-0
  1. Great Britain – Ethnic relations.   2. Great Britain – Race
relations.   3. Minorities – Great Britain.   4. Ethnology – Great
Britain.   5. Racism – Great Britain.   I. Title.   II. Series.
DA125.A1036   1991
305.8′00941 – dc20

91-11873
CIP

Contents

Acknowledgements

I would like to thank Murray Morison, the series editor, and Rob Moore, of Homerton College, for their constructive comments on the first draft of this book. I am grateful to Annette Blake for typing the final manuscript so efficiently and to Sandra den Hertog for her work on an earlier draft.

We are grateful to the following for permission to reproduce copyright material:

Croom Helm Ltd for an extract from *Multicultural Classroom* by L. Cohen & L. Manion; Gower Publishing Group for an extract from *Britain's Black Population* (1989) by B. Ashok et al. pubd. Avebury; International Thomson Publishing Services Ltd for extracts from *Colonial Immigrants in a British City: a Class Analysis* ed. Rex & Tomlinson. pubd. Routledge; Open University Press for extracts from *Young, Gifted and Black* by Mairtin Mac an Ghaill (1988); The Statesman and Nation Publishing Co Ltd for an extract from the article 'The New Racism' by A. Sivanandan in *New Statesman and Society* 4.11.88; The Times Supplements Ltd for an extract from the article 'The School Effect' in *The Times Educational Supplement* 30.6.89. Guardian News Service Ltd, Fig. 6.1, 9.3; The Harris Research Centre, Fig. 8.1; The Controller of Her Majesty's Stationery Office, Table 9.1; *New Statesman and Society*, Fig. 9.1; Office of Population Census and Surveys, Table 3.1 from *OPCS Population Trends 46*, HMSO, 1986; The Open University, Table 2.1 'Types of racial and ethnic situation' from *Race and Ethnicity* by John Rex, Open University Press, 1986; The Open University, Table 3.2, table from *OU Course E 354*, Block 2, Unit 5; Penguin Books Ltd, Fig. 9.4, table from 'Likelihood of going to prison' from *What is to be Done about Law and Order?* by J. Lea and J. Young (Penguin Books in association with the Socialist Society, 1984), copyright © John Lea and Jock Young, 1984; Policy Studies Institute, Fig. 4.5.

Series introduction

Sociology in Focus aims to provide an up-to-date, coherent coverage of the main topics that arise on an introductory course in sociology. While the intention is to do justice to the intricacy and complexity of current issues in sociology, the style of writing has deliberately been kept simple. This is to ensure that the student coming to these ideas for the first time need not become lost in what can appear initially as jargon.

Each book in the series is designed to show something of the purpose of sociology and the craft of the sociologist. Throughout the different topic areas the interplay of theory, methodology and social policy have been highlighted, so that rather than sociology appearing as an unwieldy collection of facts, the student will be able to grasp something of the process whereby sociological understanding is developed. The format of the books is broadly the same throughout. Part 1 provides an overview of the topic as a whole. In Part 2 the relevant research is set in the context of the theoretical, methodological and policy issues. The student is encouraged to make his or her own assessment of the various arguments, drawing on the statistical and reference material provided both here and at the end of the book. The final part of the book contains both statistical material and a number of 'Readings'. Questions have been provided in this section to direct students to analyse the materials presented in terms of both theoretical assumptions and methodological approaches. It is intended that this format should enable students to exercise their own sociological imaginations rather than to see sociology as a collection of universally accepted facts, which just have to be learned.

While each book in the series is complete within itself, the similarity of format ensures that the series as a whole provides an integrated and balanced introduction to sociology. It is intended that the text can be used both for individual and classroom study while the inclusion of the varied statistical and documentary materials lend themselves to both the preparation of essays and brief seminars.

To mixed race Britain: all of us

PART 1

Introduction and overview

1 Introduction

This book is about racism and racial equality. Ethnic as well as racial discrimination and prejudice are also discussed, if indeed, the two can satisfactorily be distinguished. Racism in Britain and opposition to it are the main focus of analysis. These twin themes are pursued first historically in relation to the British Empire and the post-imperial immigration into Britain and then in the more recent context of employment, housing and education. There follows a chapter on multicultural issues and their relationship to the issue of 'race'. The penultimate chapter examines race and the law and the concluding one analyses the politics of race.

In matters of race and ethnicity, Britain is very much part of the international context and this is made apparent throughout this book. As we move towards the end of the second millennium, there seems to be an increase in racial and ethnic issues across the globe. Ironically, this is partly the result of the loosening of old orders and the greater freedom people have to express their differences as well as common interests. In the Soviet Union, liberalisation has allowed multiple ethnic stirrings. In South Africa, progress towards the ending of apartheid has been laced with racial and ethnic violence and unrest. As Europe moves towards a fully free market and perhaps some form of democratic political union, several states have experienced a sharpening of xenophobia and racism against immigrant or sometimes longer-established ethnic groups. In France, for instance, support for Le Pen's National Front Party has been as high as 16 per cent against a background of anti-Jewish incidents and widespread anti-immigrant feeling.

Britain is greatly affected by the global cross-currents of racial and ethnic issues and development. This reflects its past – as the centre of a world empire – and its present aspirations – to reach outwards towards Europe and further beyond to the 'emerging world', much of which views British and Western culture with mixed feelings.

2 Terminology

Race and ethnicity

This chapter will begin by making a simple and still widely accepted distinction between 'race' and 'ethnicity'. However, objections to the use of these terms will then be discussed and an alternative reviewed.

'Race', understood in biological terms, has proved remarkably unsuccessful as a basis for categorising people and of explaining differences in their behaviour. However, this has not stopped people seeking explanations of others' behaviour in terms of their supposed race. Jews, Africans, English (by the Chinese) – indeed, perhaps every such group has been considered at one time or another 'inferior' by another group which, in turn, considered itself 'superior'. The sociology of race is largely about why people create these myths of superiority and inferiority around notions of racial difference. It is not about 'biological race' as such.

The phrase 'notions of racial difference' is used advisedly. The biological basis for belief in racial superiority and inferiority has been dismissed by the scientific community as wholly unconvincing. After the Second World War, because of the racist and, indeed, genocidal nature of Nazism, there was a widely felt need to examine the actual basis of racial differences. The United Nations commissioned various biologists and social scientists to analyse and define the meaning of race. The biologists concluded that the human species had a single origin and that *so-called* races were distinguishable by the greater statistical likelihood of their members having certain physical characteristics, such as skin colour or hair type, but these characteristics overlapped between groups. Psychological and behavioural differences were not thought to correlate with the physical ones. The biologists concluded that there is no good biological reason for one racial group treating another as inferior (as the Nazis had treated the Jews). One might add that even if there were biological differences between the 'races' which influenced behaviour, it is inconceivable that these would justify the enslavement of Africans by Western Europeans or the attempted genocide of the Jews by the Nazis – or, for that matter, any other act of racial persecution.

It is doubtful if, when people refer to 'race' in everyday life, they give much thought to whether the concept is scientifically based or not. Yet, popular – or, to use Michael Banton's term, 'folk' – usages of the term 'race' abound. It is easy to appreciate how a group perceived as physically distinct might also become popularly associated with certain patterns of behaviour. Thus, certain characteristics (usually negative) have been associated with, for instance, the Irish, Jews and Pakistanis and, in a vague way, these have sometimes been attributed to 'race'.

Clearly, then, theories – whether 'scientific' or 'folk' – of racial superiority and inferiority are the product of something other than simply dispassionate biological analysis. As we shall see shortly, sociologists examine all such 'theories' in the social context within which they occur, and, in particular, in terms of how a belief by one group in another group's 'inferiority' may be used to 'justify' exploiting it.

Whereas the sociology of race focuses on ideological invention and myth, the concept of ethnicity refers to a real phenomenon. According to Duncan Mitchell, the term denotes membership of a distinct people possessing their own customary ways or culture. He goes on to illustrate this:

> The Germans, the Jews, the Gypsies are all ethnic groups, so also Congo pygmies and Trobrianders. It will be observed that the characteristics identifying an ethnic group or aggregate may include a common language, common customs and beliefs and certainly a cultural tradition.
>
> (G. Duncan Mitchell, *A New Dictionary of Sociology*, Routledge & Kegan Paul, 1976)

Of course, all the aspects of ethnicity referred to above can change – often because of the influence of one ethnic group on another. For instance, as we shall see in the next chapter, English culture has been constantly changed as various ethnic groups have come to settle.

There can be no doubt about the growing importance of ethnicity in the contemporary world and of the immediate potential for an increase in ethnic conflict. This is partly explainable by two processes. First, the scale of international migration increased considerably during the post-Second World War period. In particular, millions of people from the underdeveloped world and Eastern Europe migrated to Western Europe (although this immigration has been increasingly sharply controlled). The United States, too, has been the focus of similar migration – much of it temporary and illegal from Mexico. This international movement of differing cultural and often linguistic groups provides the possibility of conflict (as well as cooperation and mutual benefit). In Britain, the ongoing saga of Salman Rushdie's disagreement with members of the Muslim community (in which he is accused of blasphemy in his book *The Satanic Verses*, see pages 85–8) highlights the potential for profound and seemingly irreconcilable cultural conflict.

The second process which may lead, at least in the short term, to more ethnic conflict is the liberalisation occurring in several parts of the world but notably in the Soviet Union and Eastern Europe and in South Africa. A number of ethnic groups in the Soviet Union – from Latvia to Georgia – have demanded more independence, in some case, full national independence. In South Africa, ethnic and tribal disagreements within both black and white 'communities' have surfaced as more freedom of expression has been won and rapid change occurs.

John Stone suggests that there are 'several reasons why a rigid distinction between racial and ethnic groupings can be positively misleading'. Most importantly, perhaps, is that 'racial and ethnic characteristics often overlap in any one group' (*Racial Conflict in Contemporary Society*, Fontana, 1985). Thus, the Jews have been defined in both racial and ethnic terms. A second point is that physical appearance may be a very vague and uncertain marker of a *supposedly* inferior group – the Jews in Germany are again a relevant example. It is worth adding that an additional problem for Marxists in employing the term 'ethnic' is that it suggests a misleading degree of community and common culture among groups invariably divided by class factors. Thus, there are considerable differences of wealth and life-style among British-Indians.

Stone goes on to say: 'While racial and ethnic groups may be distinguished by whether the boundary is marked out in physical or cultural terms, some would argue that the concept of a "minority" is a better tool to use in the analysis of race and ethnic relations.'

Louis Wirth's definition of the term 'minority' indicates its main characteristics: '[A minority is a] group of people distinguished by physical or cultural characteristics subject to different and unequal treatment by the society in which they live and who regard themselves as victims of collective discrimination' (Wirth, 1945, cited in Stone, 1985). A minority presupposes a majority or, at least, a more powerful or dominant group which is perceived as oppressive.

This book will use the term 'minority' where appropriate to refer to what were described above as a 'racial' or 'ethnic' group, but sometimes the compound 'racial/ethnic' is used. Where the terms 'racial' or 'ethnic' occur, it is to indicate that the minority in question is perceived by others mainly in physical or cultural terms, respectively.

Racism

In defining racism, it will be helpful to begin with a definition which covers the minimum area upon which leading authorities agree. The Marxist Robert Miles provides such a definition. He limits the meaning of racism to describe adherence to belief systems which are based on the premise that there are certain *biological* or 'natural' differences between so-called 'racial' groups on the basis of which cultural differences are considered to develop. Those who adhere to such beliefs are racist. As he puts it:

> We can . . . define racism as any set of claims or arguments which signify some aspect of the physical features of an individual or group as a sign of permanent distinctiveness and which attribute additional, negative characteristics and/or consequences to the individual's or group's presence.
>
> (Miles, 'Racism, ideology and disadvantage', in *Social Studies Review*, 5 (4), March 1990, p. 149)

The concluding part of Miles's definition referring to the attribution of 'negative characteristics' by racists to others simply means that racists regard the culture – indeed, the very 'presence', – of a given group in a negative way (because of its *supposed* racial characteristics). In short, then, Miles regards racism as *ideology* founded on the 'mistaken' division of the human species into permanent biological groups.

Miles uses the term 'racialisation' to describe the categorisation of a given individual or group on the basis of mistaken 'racial' criteria. To use his own terms: 'with respect of racialisation, "races" are not real, biological divisions of the human species but "ideological construction[s]"'. Thus, Jews and Africans have been the subject of many (sometimes contradictory) ideological constructions based on spurious biology. There is a practical as well as an ideological aspect to racialisation. Usually, in a society in which racialisation occurs, the negatively characterised group is disadvantaged in law and in access to power and resources: as, in fact, the Jews were in Nazi Germany and as black South Africans still are.

Miles's definition of racism is a very minimal one. It does not even insist that the notion of a superior and inferior group must be an aspect of racism, although it does require that one group is 'negatively characterised'.

In the 1980s and early nineties, a broader definition of racism than Miles's was adopted by several authorities. The term 'cultural racism' is sometimes used to refer to the perspective that prejudice and discrimination against individuals and groups can occur on the basis of their way of life or culture, not merely because of their biology. Barker, for example, observes that in the 1980s some Conservatives began to argue that certain 'natural' differences exist between peoples or nations and that boundaries between them ought to be maintained. They received a lead from Margaret Thatcher in this respect who, in 1979, referred to the fear that immigrants might 'swamp' the culture of 'our own people'.

John Rex can be placed within the group of theorists who consider that racism need not be founded exclusively on biological theory but sometimes is based on another kind of 'deterministic theory', including cultural. However, in his more recent book, *Race and Ethnicity* (Open University Press, 1986), Rex makes a particularly sharp distinction between racial (physical) and ethnic (cultural) situations – though not in a way that would win over his Marxist critics. In Table 2.1, Rex distinguishes between, on the one hand, racial conflict/harmony between groups and, on the other, ethnic conflict/harmony. Marxists, however, reject the idea that racial groups can be precisely established and, therefore, reject the empirical reality of 'racial' conflict/harmony. Because groups believe they are 'racial' and perhaps act in a racist way doesn't actually make them a racial group. For instance, despite thinking of themselves as 'racially pure' many white South Africans are of mixed 'race'.

Table 2.1

	Conflict situations	Situations of relative harmony
Group distinction on basis of physical (phenotypical) characteristics	Racial conflict A	Racial cooperation or interaction B
Group distinction on basis of cultural characteristics	Ethnic conflict C	Ethnic cooperation or interaction D

Source: John Rex, *Race and Ethnicity*, Open University Press, 1986, p. 22

Because of its imprecision, therefore, Marxists would require the term 'racial' to be put in inverted commas in Table 2.1. However, Rex's reminder that although ethnic conflict *may* have a racist aspect, it need not do so, is a useful one.

Institutional racism

Institutional racism is a controversial concept which has been variously defined. An early distinction between *individual* and *institutional* racism was made by black activists Stokely Carmichael and Charles Hamilton, in their book *Black Power* (1969). They describe individual racism as personal in nature, involving perpetrators and victims such as when 'a black family moves into a home in a white neighbourhood and is stoned, burned, or routed out'. They describe institutional racism as the product of the 'pervasive operation of anti-black attitudes and practices' which contribute to a pattern of black disadvantage in major areas of social life – such as health, housing and employment.

Those who have adopted the concept of institutional racism have tended particularly to stress that racist institutional 'practices' – more generally referred to as rules and procedures – can help reproduce racial inequality. However, because racial discrimination in the main areas of public life is illegal in Britain and the United States, the concept has been especially used to analyse what may variously be indirect, unconscious, unintentional and/or covert (hidden) racist practices. John Rex cites what he regards as a good example of institutional racism: the way in which public rented housing accommodation was sometimes allocated in the 1960s. Although there were seldom rules directly discriminating against black people in public housing allocation, there were several which indirectly discriminated. Thus, there were rules against considering applications from those who had recently arrived in the local authority area.

> There were also rules about overcrowding, which prevented the allocation of houses to large families. The first of these sets of rules, but the second to some extent, had the *effect* of preventing the allocation of houses to black families. The problem then was one of indirect discrimination. Quite essential to fighting institutional racism then was the task of combating such indirect discrimination.
>
> (From John Rex, *Race and Ethnicity*, p. 112)

Robert Miles has attempted to trim back definitions of institutional racism. He suggests 'a more precise definition so that it refers to two sets of circumstances'. The first refers to racist practices which may no longer be justified by openly racist arguments. He contends that British immigration law is an example of this. The second set of circumstances is when racist arguments were originally used but have been replaced by more neutral, apparently non-racist arguments. Thus, in the 1950s MPs agitating for immigration legislation wanted it to apply exclusively to 'coloured people', whereas in the 1980s and 1990s the term 'immigrants' (meaning 'coloured immigrants') was more common.

It is easy to imagine that Miles's first usage of 'institutional racism' will gain wider acceptance. No doubt to his chagrin, however, it is likely to be added to rather than replace existing usages of the concept. This is because the broader concept of institutional racism has already influenced anti-racist policy and is likely to continue to do so (see page 74).

Racism and racialism: an unnecessary distinction?

John Rex makes a distinction between racism and racialism: 'Racism refer[s] to theory, racialism to practice.' In other words, he makes a distinction between ideology (racism) and behaviour (racialism).

The relevance of this distinction is particularly apparent in

Figure 2.1 **Definitions and measures of racism**
The table below provides more information about individual and institutional racism. Both forms of racism are presented in attitudinal and related behavioural terms. The material describing individual racism is straightforward, but some of the terms associated with institutional racism are quite complex. Thus, an institutional *symbol* of racism would be the Nazi swastika; a racist myth, that of white supremacy. The behavioural aspects of institutional racism refer to the practical ways in which it is implemented and maintained.

	Attitudinal	*Behavioural*
Individual	Personal attitudes, opinions, values	Personal acts, behaviours, choices or non-choices
Institutional	Organisation/societal norms, symbols, fashions, myths	Organisational/societal procedures, programmes, mechanisms

Source: Adapted from M. Chester and H. Delgado, 'Race relations training and organisational change', in John W. Shaw *et al.*, *Strategies for Improving Race Relations: The Anglo-American Experience*, Manchester University Press, 1987, p. 185

considering how to combat 'racism/racialism'. Attitudes and beliefs (racism) can sometimes be changed through socialisation, including education, whereas behaviour (racialism) can be dealt with more immediately by the law; namely, by making some forms of discrimination illegal. In Britain, race relations legislation has been aimed mainly at preventing discriminatory behaviour in major areas of public life.

However, many authorities refer simply to racist beliefs, attitudes and ideology, on the one hand, and racist behaviour, on the other. For instance, in Figure 2.1 the term 'racism' refers to both attitudes and behaviour. Certainly, a problem for Rex is that the term 'institutional racism' – which he adopts – includes behaviour as well as beliefs and attitudes.

The distinction between prejudice and discrimination similarly reflects that between beliefs and behaviour. Prejudice refers to 'learned *beliefs and values* that lead an individual or group of individuals to be biased for or against members of particular groups', whereas 'discrimination is the unfavourable *treatment* of all persons socially assigned to a particular category' (E. E. Cashmore, *Dictionary of Race and Ethnic Relations*, Routledge, 1988 – my italics).

Racial equality

Two broad perspectives on racial equality can be distinguished: the liberal and the socialist. The liberal view is based on the belief that all people, regardless of race, are entitled to basic human rights. Generally, these are considered to be civil (legal), political and social (that is, including some social welfare rights). Equal rights and opportunity under the law is not taken to mean that everybody will reach a similar situation in society (equality of outcome). Rather, the liberal emphasis is that 'the rules should be fair' and that there is no discrimination against any particular group.

The black civil rights movement in the United States is a classic example of an attempt (successful) to achieve racial equality under the law. The Civil Rights Act 1964 made illegal discrimination in the main public areas of American life, including housing and employment. The Voting Rights Act 1965 reinforced equal political rights between the races. The American civil rights movement and civil rights legislation have stood as an example of liberal action for racial equality.

Socialist perspective on equality argues that people should be much more equal in the material and cultural resources available to them than they are under capitalism. This commitment to greater equality of resources is regardless of race. Whereas the liberal concept of equality of opportunity stresses 'fair competition', from which individuals may emerge unequal, the socialist approach contends that society should be organised so that large inequalities do not develop and so that individual and group needs are met as adequately as possible. Again, the socialist approach is 'colour blind' in that it applies equally to all. Socialists argue that the main strategy for achieving greater equality is through class action, which transcends supposed racial differences. The most effective way in which black and white working-class people can improve their situation is to act together. However, socialists recognise that racism does occur and argue that victims of it may need to organise as a district group *within* a wider socialist frame-

Figure 2.2 The liberal view of racism and racial equality

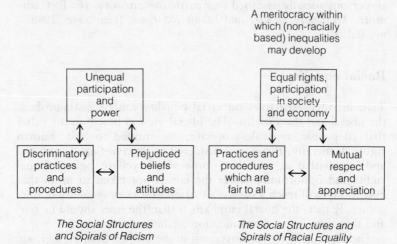

Source: Adapted from a model in a Berkshire County Council policy paper, reprinted in the Swann Report, *Education for All*, p. 370

work. Thus, some socialists argue that there should be black sections *within* multiracial socialist parties.

The use of the term 'black'

In this book, the term 'black' will be used to describe groups of people of African and Asian origin although, of course, more specific terms such as 'Afro-Caribbean' (or, sometimes, 'West Indian') and 'British-Asian' will be used where appropriate.

Such a wide usage of the term 'black' may surprise some readers. For many of African and Asian origin, the term 'black' has been adopted as a matter of pride and positive self-identity. In the 1960s, politically active Afro-Americans and Afro-Britons often rejected the terms 'negro' and 'coloured' as being white people's way of referring to them. They considered that these terms had acquired negative associations implying that they were inferior. 'Black' became their own choice of term, and they insist that 'black is beautiful' and assert the reality of 'black power'. The self-description 'black' came to imply a rejection of racism and inferiority and an assertion of positive self-identity. Many politically conscious people of Asian origin also adopted the self-description 'black' for the same kind of reasons. Thus, the term further came to imply Afro-Asian solidarity in rejecting racism and asserting positive self-identity.

The above reasons are sufficient to justify the continued broad usage of the term 'black' adopted here. However, there is a major difficulty in currently using the term. This is because, despite their *common* experience of racism and opposing racism, people of African and Asian origin are often very different from one another (these differences occur within as well as between the two major groupings). Great differences occur in all major areas of life – economic, social and cultural – and the use of the term 'black' must not be allowed to hide these. As Malcolm Cross writes:

> [T]here is an understandable reluctance to abandoning the term 'black' as a political label uniting all minorities in a common struggle against racism. But many Asians and Afro-Caribbeans are rejecting the term because it presents a false, dangerously simple homogeneity [i.e., sameness].
> (Malcolm Cross, 'Moving targets: the changing face of racism', *New Society*, 7 April 1989, p. 35)

It may be that in ten years or so the term 'black' will have been replaced – perhaps by several terms – but for the moment it will be used here.

Explanations of racism

This section briefly reviews some theories as to the reasons for the existence of racism. Why is it that prejudice and discrimination expressed in terms of 'race' are so widespread?

It will help to look at this issue – the key in the area of 'race' relations – in both individual and societal terms. It may well be that certain individual personality types are more prone to racism than others but equally some societies are more racist than others. Any satisfactory sociological explanation of racism must effectively address differences at the societal level. What is needed is not merely an explanation of why certain extreme personality type(s) may be prone to racism but why, in some societies, many ordinary people are racist. This section proceeds from psychological, through social psychological, to sociological explanations of racism, matching the individual/societal focus.

Psychological

Among the best-known analyses of racism based on individual psychology is Adorno's theory of the *authoritarian personality*. Adorno particularly wanted to explain the racism against and, indeed, attempted genocide of the Jews in Germany.

According to Adorno, the authoritarian personality is likely to be formed as a result of a particular pattern of socialisation. This is a combination of strictness about observing rules with little outlet to express feelings of resentment against being ordered about. Without realising it, authoritarian personalities tend to look for *scapegoats* against whom they can express both moral disapproval and frustrated aggression. In Adorno's view, anti-Semitism in inter-war Germany was a case of such scapegoating. Research by Pettigrew in the southern United States and in South Africa did find a positive correlation between authoritarianism and anti-Semitism but not with racism against black people. It was clear that racism in these societies extended well beyond a single personality type and that a satisfactory explanation of widespread racism in the American South is required to be sought in the history and culture of the area. As we shall see, such a broader explanation is relevant to European, including British, racism, although it is quite possible that certain personality types are more prone to racism than others.

Social psychological

Granted, as sociologists argue, that the particular form(s) racism takes in a given society depends on historical context, there is still a need to explain why groups, societies even, become more or less racist so easily and frequently. What is it about inter-group relations that can lead to racism? There is considerable agreement among social psychologists and sociologists that the need of individuals to *categorise* people into groups to which ego (self) 'belongs' and groups to which ego does not 'belong' is universal. Groups to which an individual belongs are family and 'tribe' or nation. It is not inevitable that the individual will have negative relations with groups to which he or she does not belong. However, conflict with such groups is certainly possible. Social psychologist Henri Tajfel suggests how such conflict can lead to negative categorisation of the 'other'.

For Tajfel, an individual's society identity is defined as 'that part of an individual's self-concept which derives from his [sic] knowledge of his membership of a social group (or groups) together with the emotional significance attached to that membership' (H. Tajfel, *The Social Psychology of Minorities*, Minorities Rights Group, 1978). Citing relevant empirical research, he argues that members of groups (in-groups) – from families to societies – continually compare themselves with other groups (out-groups) in the same category (for example, members of a society compare their society with others). In general, members of a given group tend to value their own group characteristics more highly than those of other groups. In other words, they tend to see their own group as 'superior' and other groups as 'inferior'. However, a group that is in a powerful position in relation to another group may be able to persuade members of the less powerful group that their group *is* inferior. According to Tajfel, *negative stereotyping* (that is, crude caricaturing) of the so-called 'inferior' group helps to maintain the 'superior–inferior' relationships. Thus, white stereotypes of blacks as 'stupid' or 'good entertainers' serve to 'keep them in their place'.

The application of Tajfel's theory to an indigenous majority population (for example, white Britons) and an ethnic minority (such as British-Asians) is obvious. An indigenous majority may assert its 'superiority' in a variety of ways, although minority members may or may not accept the majority definition.

Charles Husband has argued that Tajfel's theory of inter-group relations is helpful in understanding race relations provided that each race relations situation is fully analysed in its *historical/social* context (Husband, 'Race, identity and British society', Open University course material, 1982). The possible variations in power relations between majority and minority groups and of the responses between them are so great that Tajfel's approach provides no more than a general guide.

Sociological

In examining racism, this book draws mainly on two sociological traditions: those initiated by Weber and Marx. Contemporary Weberian John Rex and contemporary Marxist Robert Miles appear to agree on two important aspects of racism. First, racism is a form of ideology based on the view that the human species can be divided into 'naturally' differing groups which must, as a consequence, be socially differentiated. Racist ideology involves a negative evaluation of others in comparison with one's own group. Second, the particular form racism takes reflects given social structural realities. Because each historical occurrence of racism is to some extent unique, Miles and others have begun to use the term 'racisms'. Both points will be briefly examined in turn.

Rex defines racism in essentially ideological terms as follows: 'Racism involve[s] belief systems which suggest that a category of individuals [is] for some sort of deterministic reason (usually biological) incapable of moving from one social position to another' (1986, p. 119).

In his following comparison of racism to similarly based ideologies Miles insists more strongly than Rex on its biological reductionism: 'As an ideology, racism shares certain characteristics with others [that is, ideologies, such as sexism]. . . . The central shared characteristic is the mistaken postulation of natural divisions within the human species which are defined as inherent and universal. These divisions are therefore, presented as inevitable determinants of social organisation' (Miles, 1989, p. 87).

Examples abound of racism as a form of ideological justification. In South Africa the Bible has been used by whites as a source to 'explain' the 'inferiority' of black people – and so the exploitation of their labour and denial of their rights. More usually evolutionary theories have been referred to in order to justify exploiting, stereotyping and scapegoating a particular 'racial' group. A rather blatant example of this occurred in the *Encyclopaedia Britannica* for 1884:

> No full-blooded Negro has ever been distinguished as a man of science, a poet, or an artist, and the fundamental inequality claimed for him by ignorant philanthropists is belied by the whole history of the race.

In contrast, racism against Jews has usually focused on imagined moral rather than intellectual 'inferiority'. Within Nazi *cosmology* (total system of explanation/reference), Jews were characterised as 'evil' as distinct from Aryans who were depicted as 'pure'. Thus, the Nazis partly 'explained' the German economic crisis of the 1920s by supposed Jewish business profiteering (the Jews were also blamed for the rise of Communism in Germany and for the 'Communist world conspiracy'!). The ideological demeaning of the Jews served to 'justify' the Nazis' material pillage of them.

We now turn to the second point on which Rex and Miles agree: that the particular form racism takes reflects given social structural realities. In the following references to racism in the United States and Britain, he is very specific in indicating the practical circumstances stimulating racism (although he also acknowledges the carry-over effect of previous racism):

> In the United States there was not only the historical legacy of a slave-plantation society, but Black migrants from that society were seeking to compete for employment and housing with White Americans and White immigrants in the North. . . . [I]n Britain, there was a legacy of a colonial society in which colonized people were regarded as inferior, and an industrial and social structure on which socially mobile Whites had abandoned jobs and other social positions and Black workers were brought in to fill these positions. The problems were not those which arose from racism either on the psychological or the theoretical level, but questions of social structure and inequality.
> (Rex, 1986, p. 105)

Miles further describes the interplay of racist ideology and practical circumstances (in this case, mainly economic) in referring to the post-war immigration of black people into Britain:

> Since the 1950s, the British labour market has been racialised in this way. Employers have signified certain physical and cultural characteristics (notably skin colour, and hence the designation 'coloured labour' or 'coloured workers') of Caribbean and Asian migrants and their British-born children, and this signification has structured recruitment processes. They believed not only that the labour market consisted of a number of different 'races' but also that these 'races' had different characteristics which influenced their employability. . . .
> What were the reasons for this exclusionary practice? Part of the explanation lies in the fact that the majority of migrants, including those who considered themselves skilled in the

context of the forces and relations of production in the Carib-bean and the Indian subcontinent, had few skills relevant to an industrial capitalist economy, and, on this criterion, were likely to be excluded from any form of skilled manual or non-manual employment. But racism was also a motivating factor. Some employers explained their exclusionary practices by reference to the anticipated or real opposition of their existing workforce to working with 'coloureds', opposition that they endorsed by act-ing in this manner. Others negatively stereotyped Asians as 'slow to learn', or West Indians as lazy, unresponsive to disci-pline and truculent, or 'coloured people' generally as prone to accidents or requiring more supervision than 'white' workers. In all these instances, migrants were signified by skin colour and attributed collectively with negatively evaluated characteristics. Not all employers in Wright's survey articulated such racist views and so unanimity should not be assumed.

(Miles, 1989)

At this point no assumptions are being made about exactly how Miles or Rex explain the relationship between racist ideology and the economy. What is clear is that, like Rex, Miles sees a complex interaction between racist ideology and socio-economic structure. The nature of this interaction is the subject matter of the next two chapters.

Race and ethnicity in Britain

3 Immigration, culture and racism in Britain

Whereas the first part of this book was largely theoretical, Part 2 makes a concrete examination of race and ethnic relations in Britain, particularly England.

The early part of this chapter deals mainly with the motives behind Britain's imperial expansion – which brought Britons into contact with black people – and with post-Second World War immigration into Britain. The middle section of the chapter examines the settlement of black people in Britain and concentrates mainly on the issues of ethnic negotiation/adjustment and racism. The third section analyses some of the varieties of British racism, and particularly the influence of historical and class factors on racism.

Britain in the world and the world in Britain

Britain in the world

The three 'c's' – commerce, conquest and conversion (to Christianity) – are often cited as the main motives which prompted Britons and other Europeans to travel the globe. Scientific curiosity was another motive. In some cases, notably Australia, other parts of the world were used as dumping grounds for Britain's criminal classes. However, far more emigrated from Britain of their own free will, establishing English-speaking societies throughout the world.

The extent of British power and influence in modern history has been great, even though it has been eclipsed by that of the United States and the Soviet Union in the post-Second World War period. The formal Empire – that is, areas directly ruled by Britain – amounted to about a quarter of the world's land surface when the Empire was at its height – and this was *after* the North American colonies had gained independence. Many other large areas of the world were either wholly or partly under British commercial domination, including parts of South America and China.

The world in Britain

Many people have migrated to Britain because of the links which had been made by Britons with their countries. As early as 1555, five Africans were brought to Britain by a merchant to be taught English so that they could act as interpreters for British traders with Africa. Throughout the nineteenth and twentieth centuries, many millions of people visited or settled in Britain as a result of the links first established with their countries by Britons. In the nineteenth century, the Irish and Jews from Eastern Europe were among the main immigrant groups. However, the flow of people in and out of Britain began many hundreds of years ago – probably several millennia – before Britain became a world power. Centuries of immigration into and settlement in Britain mean that Britain has been multi-ethnic for all, or virtually all, of its recorded history.

Britain's first recognisable black communities had been established by the late eighteenth century, perhaps altogether about 10,000 people. Throughout the nineteenth century, black communities developed in the former slave-trade ports of London, Bristol and Liverpool (the slave-trade in the British Empire was abolished in 1806 and slavery itself in 1833).

However, it was after the Second World War that the vast majority of black immigration into Britain occurred. According to figures published by the Office of Population Censuses and Surveys (OPCS), the percentage of Britain's non-white minorities of the total population in 1951 was 0.4, whereas by 1985 it was approximately 4.3. By 1985, 50 per cent of those of Caribbean origin had been born in Britain, and by the early nineties, the percentage for the total non-white minorities must be about that figure. The great majority of children of Caribbean and Asian origin were born in Britain. Table 3.1 gives details of the size of the larger non-white minorities in Britain in 1983–85.

Table 3.1 *Minority populations in Great Britain, 1983–85 (average)*

	Number (thousands)	Percentage born in UK
Caribbean	530	50
Indian	760	35
Pakistani	380	40
Bangladeshi	90	30
African	100	35
Chinese	110	20
Arab	60	10
Mixed origin	210	75
Other	100	25
Total non-white	2,350	40

Source: Office of Population Censuses and Surveys, 1986

Empire and after: the economic logic

The Empire gave Britain access to cheap natural and human resources (including slaves) and to vast markets for manufactured
products. Ali Rattansi makes the further point that the British and
other European empires left a degree of inequality between themselves and the societies they dominated which had consequences
beyond the formal break-up of the empires. In particular, he
stresses the 'pools' of labour available partly as a result of
underdevelopment:

> There is a maldistribution of world wealth and income such that
> the countries of the Northern hemisphere contain only 25 per
> cent of the world's population but obtain 80 per cent of the
> world's income, while the countries of the South contain 75 per
> cent of the world's population but obtain only 20 per cent of
> the world's income.
>
> This profound asymmetry in the structure and evolution of
> the world economic system provides the essential background
> to the more recent migrations of black communities to Britain
> in the post-Second World War period, for one of its main effects
> has been the creation of pools of under- and unemployed work-
> ers in circumstances of poverty and restricted opportunity in the
> Third World, who find themselves having to undergo the

painful dislocation entailed by migration and travel thousands
of miles in search of work.

(A. Rattansi, 'Race, education and British society', in R. Dale
et al., Frameworks for Teaching, Falmer Press, 1985, p. 248)

Poverty and lack of employment opportunity provided what
Peach refers to as the 'push' factors behind migration from the
New Commonwealth countries (C. Peach, *West Indian Migration
to Britain*, OUP for the Institute of Race Relations, 1968).

Equally important were the 'pull' factors exerted from Britain.
In the immediate post-war period the British economy was
undergoing expansion and restructuring (radical changes) which
required the availability of a supply of cheap, flexible labour. This
was mainly needed in heavy manufacturing and transport but also
in the National Health Service. Among other government agencies, the Ministry of Health under Enoch Powell advertised for
nurses in Caribbean countries. At the same time, there was a rapid
growth of the service sector of the economy, both public and private – which provided millions of new white-collar jobs. For a
variety of reasons, including racism and lack of relevant experience
and qualifications among some black immigrants, these jobs went
almost exclusively to white people in the early post-war period.
Thus, many white people moved up to service-sector jobs, while
black people replaced them in mainly manual work.

A number of Marxist sociologists have developed and illustrated
the reserve pool or 'army' of labour theory. These include Castles
and Kosack (1973) and Miles (1989). Easily hired when needed
and fired when not, the reserve pool greatly facilitates the development of capitalism. However, both Castles and Kosack and
Miles stress that the reserve pool need not be of any particular
colour (or, for that matter, sex or age). Its main characteristic is
that it is highly open to manipulation: in other words, it is
'flexible'. Both explore the existence and functioning of reserve
pools of labour in relation to other parts of the world, particularly
the so-called 'guest workers' of West Germany. They argue that
because West Germany expanded more rapidly than Britain during
most of the post-war period, its demand for reserve labour was
correspondingly greater. In West Germany, prior to unification,
the migrant population was about 3 million, including over a million Turks – a somewhat greater proportion of the country's total
population than the approximately 2 million black immigrants

(including later offspring) into Britain are of Britain's total population.

John Rex and Sally Tomlinson broadly agree with the analysis of the economic motives behind the immigration of black people into Britain referred to above. However, they argue that black immigrants experience racial disadvantage in addition to possible class disadvantage. Moreover, as they indicate in the following passage, certain working–class people as well as certain middle-class people are racist in Britain (as they are in South Africa, Rex's country of origin). Rex, therefore, follows Weber's analysis that racism is a form of status differentiation which, whilst it may interact with class differentiation, is distinct from it and can occur separately.

A major problem in the analysis of British class structure, even before the arrival of immigrants from the former colonial societies, concerns the relationship between the relatively straightforward class structure of class struggle in metropolitan society and that which prevails in the imperial social system as a whole. Oddly enough, this is a problem which has hardly been discussed in British sociology. The suggestion which we would make is that the two parts of the system, metropolitan and colonial, have been separated from each other by a caste-like barrier, and that, despite the class struggle which goes on between classes in the metropolitan sector, these classes unite in the exploitation of, and in defence against, any threat from segments or groups within or from colonial society. This notion, of course, conflicts with any simplistic Marxist expectation of the unity of the international working class, though not with the more general notion that class formation arises from men's relation to the means of production. The relevant 'means of production' here is the imperial system as a whole.

(John Rex and Sally Tomlinson *et al., Colonial Immigrants in a British City: a Class Analysis*, Routledge & Kegan Paul, 1979, p. 16)

Minorities and majority: adaptation and negotiation

Majority culture and minority subcultures

Over the centuries there has been a steady flow of immigrant groups into Britain through either military occupation or peaceful settlement. Jews and Irish, Poles and Italians, Afro-Caribbeans and Asians have all adapted to Britain (mainly England) differently, and have, of course, been received somewhat differently. As well as being changed by it, incoming minority groups have changed the existing culture. This section describes and analyses this mutual process of *adaptation* and *negotiation*. By adaptation is meant change – mainly, but not exclusively, to coexist more effectively. *Negotiation* refers to the two-way process by which minority and majority groups find, by some measure of give and take, a way of living together or not.

What is culture?

Before examining the relationship between British and minority culture, the term 'culture' itself must be defined. In common sociological usage, the concept of culture refers to a shared way of life. Raymond William adds that a shared way of life can include matters over which people conflict as well as agree. Thus, distinct groups, from the French to the Aboriginals, have their own cultures. A subculture is a minority way of life within a majority culture. Thus, Chinese-Britons have developed their own minority subculture within British culture.

What, then, are the key elements in a 'shared way of life' or 'common culture'? The following are important, if not essential, elements to a common culture:

shared language
　　　history
　　　norms and customs
　　　sense of group identity.

Culture is the product of social interaction rather than geography, but it helps to distinguish between various socio-geographical levels óf culture. Thus, distinct cultures and subcultures can occur at national, regional and local levels; for example, British, Northern, Liverpudlian. Sometimes, of course, these and other differences can be the cause of tension, disagreement and conflict in a society. Britain has the added potential for conflict and even break-up in that it is comprised of several nations: the Scottish, Irish, Welsh and English. However, forms of cultural identity, such as belonging to a particular religion (for instance, Muslim) or youth group (like Hippies) frequently cut across natural boundaries and can challenge national cultures. As an example, if Pope and Prince, or Prime Minister, disagree, whom should a Catholic obey?

Because certain people *belong* to a given cultural group and others do not, there is an inevitable element of 'us' and 'them' about cultural identity. People are unavoidably aware of cultural differences such as language and custom. Such awareness is normally accompanied by caution in relation to 'strangers', that is, members of other cultures. Cultural groups vary in the ease with which 'outsiders' can gain access to them. Thus, it is probably easier to 'become a punk' than to 'become a Hindu'. Here, our particular concern is how 'outsiders', specifically immigrants, gain access to an indigenous (existing majority) culture. Again, this varies between societies. Thus, the United States has been referred to as 'a society of immigrants', and it has probably been easier for immigrants there to 'become American' than for immigrants to a more closed society, such as China, to 'become Chinese'. We will shortly discuss the issue of 'becoming British'.

Being culturally British is quite distinct from being a British citizen. Citizenship is a legal status, carrying in its full form right of abode in a given country. In some cases, individuals may possess British citizenship without speaking English or ever having been to Britain. In most cases, however, citizens of a given country also share its culture.

British culture and nation: consensus, conflict and complexity

To what extent do the majority of Britons share the four elements of a common culture: common language, history, norms and customs and sense of group identity? On the first and second points, clearly, the majority of Britons speak English, albeit in different dialects, and possess a common history – even though they disagree about what is important within it. The third area – that of shared customs, norms and beliefs – raises more difficulties.

However, it is evident that in everyday life, Britons have enough customs and norms in common to create a reasonably effective society. A non-Briton with no knowledge of British culture – say, a Mongolian or even a Greek – would be likely to 'cope' less well and would both experience and create problems of communication. The fourth element in a common national culture, a shared sense of group identity, is partly the product of the other key elements. Sharing the language, history and everyday way of the life of a society creates a sense of belonging. Most people care for the national group they belong to, and this is perhaps the most acceptable form of patriotism. In this sense, most Britons are patriotic in the same way as members of other nations.

It must be stressed again that there is vast scope for difference and disagreement among members of the same national culture. Simply sharing the four common elements of a culture in no way ensures consensus about their meaning and use. This is especially obvious in the case of language and history, the use and interpretation of which varies enormously within national groups. Class and region, as well as ethnicity, produce differences among the British and these are expressed, in turn, in difference of dress, dialect and behaviour. Let us pursue the case of British history as an example of an element which is shared but about which people, nevertheless, disagree. Historian Jonathan Clark expresses both aspects well:

> One side [the Left] wants us [the British] to shoulder the moral burden of 18th-century slavery, the other [the Right] invites us to take the credit for 19th-century democracy and the rule of law. One praises the legacy of the Levellers, the other deplores the heritage of Marxism. . . .
>
> Patriotism is alive and well as long as such arguments go on. If so, it is unperceptive to dismiss the Left as unpatriotic or the Right as jingoistic. They both care.
>
> (*Guardian*, 18 July 1989, p. 31)

Clark is suggesting that caring for Britain is an aspect of being part of it. However, for those minority groups, now settled in Britain, which historically have suffered at the hands of the British, 'caring' may be a complicated and difficult issue.

Our account of British culture so far is open to the accusation that it somewhat emphasises cultural consensus (agreement) at the expense of conflict and complexity. This is not really so, in that while Britons do share the same language and history, it has also been emphasised here that they often use language and interpret history in ways that reflect disagreement, sometimes deep disagreement. Difference, disagreement and conflict also occur in the areas of norms and customs and group identity. The norms and customs of Eton and Cambridge and those of an inner urban comprehensive and routine place of work (entered at 16 or 17 years of age) are self-evidently very different. These differences can be the basis of antagonisms and conflicts between those who experience them – though not necessarily so. Similarly, 'group identity' in the sense of a feeling of belonging to the same nation may differ between individuals and groups (see below). Nevertheless, it seems likely that the great majority of Britons do feel part of 'the same' nation.

It is important to conceptualise more fully the bases of cultural difference and conflict within Britain. Class, age (notably in the form of 'youth cultures') and gender are familiar bases of cultural organisation – although the cultural responses of women to their experiences of patriarchy and class have, until quite recently, been neglected. Because the subject matter of this book is race and ethnicity, it is how the latter 'cross with' or interact with the other main areas of stratification (which are also the main bases of cultural organisation) that must be unravelled. Again, while race/ethnicity has been extensively analysed in relation to class and youth, it is only recently that linkages with gender have been explored.

Following Stuart Hall, Charles Husband has suggested that 'there is no single monolithic ideology' of nation 'shared by all Britons'. Rather, people have 'images' of Britain which differ and which do 'not necessarily have the same range of meaning' (Husband, 1987). The debate on the rights of British passport holders in Hong Kong to settle in Britain can be suggested as a relevant example. Those whose preferred image of Britain is of a liberal, open and racially tolerant society tend to favour a generous interpretation of rights of settlement, whereas those who, in some sense, see Britain as culturally or racially exclusive (and, perhaps, 'white') tend to favour a narrow interpretation. Paddy Ashdown is an example of the former, Norman Tebbit, of the latter.

In order to explain further the variety of attitudes to nation and race/ethnicity, Husband cites Abercrombie and Turner's critique of 'the dominant ideology thesis' (1978). The dominant ideology thesis simply states that at any given time the ideas and attitudes of 'the ruling class' are likely to be highly influential (if not overwhelmingly so) among other classes as well. Thus, Husband agrees that upper-class racism in the nineteenth century did percolate through British society and affect the attitudes and behaviour of working-class people. However, Husband also subscribes to Abercrombie and Turner's critique of the dominant ideology thesis that the situation of working-class people – often involving 'exploitation' – in the workplace and in their communities, provides an alternative fund of experience and ideas which may lead them to be critical of ruling-class ideology. Thus, there is some evidence that white working-class people with close and shared experience of black people are less likely to be racist than if they have relied exclusively on the media for information about them (see page 35). Applying the critique of the dominant ideology thesis to racial ideology, Husband argues that different bases of experience produce *racisms* rather than racism – a point which is taken up in the next section.

Marxism has traditionally been very critical of nationalism (or 'ethnicism') as a form of ideology. This is because Marxism itself is an international ideology which advocates working-class cooperation across international boundaries. Whatever the actual practice of particular Marxist regimes, ultimately Marxists aspire to an international community based not on national competition, but on the meeting of mutual needs. Robert Miles sees what he terms an 'articulation' (complementary and close relationship) between nationalism and racism (Miles, 1989). Crudely, the sort of things nationalists believe tend to be the sort of things racists believe. He draws his evidence for the frequency of this relationship from recent European history, but within Britain the National Front Party and, less formally, the views of some football 'hooligans' provide more immediate examples. In both cases, strident nationalism coexists with overt racism.

Cultural adaptation and negotiation

The arrival and settlement of minority groups in Britain is nothing new. Britain has been militarily occupied or peacefully settled by many minority groups over thousands of years. Each group has contributed to British culture. A small example is given in Figure 3.1.

Figure 3.1
The list below gives a single word contributed to the English
language by each of a number of ethnic groups:

Group	Word contributed
Celts	Celtic
Romans	ego
Anglo-Saxons	earl
Vikings	Thursday
French (Normans)	chef
Irish	Blarney
Jews	pretsel
Asians	mosques
Afro-Caribbeans	reggae

The question of how various minority groups have adapted culturally to British life now needs to be discussed. The first point
to stress is that adaptation is always, to some extent, a two-way
process: both the minority culture and the indigenous majority
culture change as they interact. Second, various minority groups
adapt in different ways. Thus, they absorb different aspects of the
majority culture – more or less quickly. These two points can be
summed up by stating that the coming together of two cultures
involves *negotiation*, with, at least, some give and take from both
sides.

The extent to which an ethnic minority culture is *absorbed* into
the majority culture can be presented in the form of a model as
follows:

Extent of ethnic minority absorption into the majority culture		
Total absorption		*No absorption*
Assimilation	Pluralism	Separatism

Minority assimilation occurs when a minority group becomes
fully absorbed into the majority culture. An example of assimilation is the case of the French Huguenots, whose descendants

today appear to have little or no ethnic identity other than perhaps some memories of their forebears.

Ethnic pluralism or integration occurs when a minority group retains its own identity and practices but also fully participates in the 'mainstream' life of a society. The Jews are good example of a group which has adapted in this way. Many continue to practise their characteristic religious and cultural rituals and behaviours whilst also working and socialising with non-Jews. Support for an ethnically pluralistic society is particularly associated with liberalism (see pages 86–8).

Some minorities retain a high degree of separate identity and life-style from the majority culture and have not become fully integrated within it. They fall between pluralism and separatism in the model. Certain groups of Asian origin tend to fit this pattern. Thus, a large number of British Bangladeshis – notably in the Tower Hamlets area of London – do not speak much English and participate relatively little in life outside their own families and ethnic community. Paid work can bring adults into regular contact with others, but high rates of unemployment cut off many from even this source of wider interaction. In Tower Hamlets, Bangladeshi children are often in the majority – or form at least a large minority of the pupils – and thus interaction with other ethnic groups is less than it might otherwise be.

Total ethnic separatism within a majority culture is virtually impossible but it is sometimes put forward as a goal by individuals or groups within minorities. There is a tradition of separatism among both some American and British blacks of Afro-Caribbean extraction. In Britain, some Rastafarians argue that a return to Africa is the only way blacks will ever achieve social justice. Separatist aspirations usually indicate a deep sense of grievance against the majority culture.

The process of negotiating their own British cultural identity has been made acutely difficult for black ethnic groups by white racism. The varieties of British 'racism' are discussed later in this chapter, and racism within British culture is analysed in Chapter 5. Some brief comments are now offered on the model of adaptation discussed above.

Comment on assimilation (the host–immigrant model), pluralism and separatism

In the fifties, many assumed that immigrants would or even should simply fit into or assimilate to what they thought of as 'the British way of life'. Rather too simply, assimilation of immigrant groups was thought to have occurred in the United States and so was expected to occur 'naturally' in Britain. American sociologists often adopted a *host–immigrant* framework to explain immigration. The model argues that immigrant groups normally go through a process of increasing adaptation to the 'host' society into which they eventually become largely assimilated. There are important criticisms of the assimilationist approach.

First, a group cannot simply *choose* precisely how its members will relate to the majority culture. How members relate will depend on a vast variety of factors, such as their education and ability and opportunity to speak and learn English and the nature of their own customs and beliefs. Thus, many Muslims do not want to adopt majority practices in relation to alcohol and sexual explicitness.

Equally important in influencing how a minority group adapts to society is how its members are treated by others. British-Italians, for instance, appear to have been easily accepted by the majority and this has helped them to prosper. On the other hand, as conflict theorists stress, the racism experienced by many black Britons has hindered their progress.

In any case, the concepts of assimilation, pluralism and separatism should be seen as models or ideal types to which most members of a particular minority group may roughly conform. There are, of course, many individuals within any minority group who do not conform to its general pattern of adaptation. Thus, some 'Jews' have assimilated rather than integrated even to the point of dropping their religion and changing their names to sound non-Jewish.

The making of race relations in post-war Britain

Both racism and racial tolerance have for long been part of British life. Historically, racism has probably been the stronger of these two cultural traditions, but in the immediate post-war period there were reasons for thinking that Britain might develop as a success-ful and largely harmonious multiracial society. The Empire was giving way to the more egalitarian Commonwealth. Blacks and whites had fought together against fascism, and this had created much goodwill between the 'races'. Certainly, the evidence is that many New Commonwealth immigrants came to Britain expect-ing not only to become better off but to be made welcome.

It did not quite work out that way. Indeed, it is easy to over-estimate even the initial goodwill of both the British government and people to the New Commonwealth immigrants. The main motive for inviting New Commonwealth immigrants to Britain was the practical one of increasing Britain's labour supply. Far less official help was extended to New Commonwealth immigrants to Britain than to the 50,000 or so Polish Second World War refu-gees. Tom Rees has referred to the Polish Resettlement Act 1947 as 'one of the few constructive legislative initiatives in the field of immigration', and it provided for substantial help in the areas of employment, housing and education.

The 'official' reason why black immigrants received no such help was that, as British citizens, they had right of access to public services. However, in fact, they were disadvantaged not only by direct racism but, in some cases, indirectly, by regulations such as residency requirements in relation to public housing.

In the private housing market, notices such as 'No blacks, no Irish, no dogs' were common. A major 'race riot' occurred in 1958 in London's Notting Hill district when, according to Edward Pilkington, Afro-Caribbeans for the first time systematically organised to defend themselves against repeated racial attacks and provocation:

> By fighting back the West Indians added a new dimension to the riots, which now threatened to escalate into full-blooded racial war. For the police this was an alarming development, caught as they were between a mass of violent white youths intent on killing 'nigs' and black people determined to defend themselves by any means necessary.
>
> (Edward Pilkington, 'White riot, a riot of their own', *Observer*, 27 August 1988)

The government response was to pass the 1962 Commonwealth Immigrants Act which was intended to have the effect of reducing black immigration. This was to be achieved by requiring an immigrant to possess a work voucher, which became increasingly difficult to obtain – for would-be black immigrants. The immediate effect of the Act was to cause a rush of black immigrants, especially from Asia, before it came into force. Many commentators have seen this Act as an example of 'punishing the victims' – especially as legislation making racial discrimination illegal only came several years later and has been less effective than immigration control (see pages 90–103).

British 'racisms': the variety of racism in Britain

During the 1980s, particularly in the latter half of the decade, there was increasing analysis of the variety of racism in Britain. The titles of the following three works give the flavour of this discussion: Ellis Cashmore. *The Logic of Racism* (1987); Charles Husband, *British Racisms: The Construction of Racial Ideologies* (1988); and Cohen and Bains (eds), *Multi-racist Britain* (1988). The term 'racisms', which is beginning to creep in, is rather cumbersome, but it is important to appreciate that the forms racism takes vary considerably. The last chapter illustrated that racism can take different forms in different cultures and that it changes historically within any one culture (see the reference to the United States for the latter point, page 17). The focus of this section is on the variety of racism within Britain.

Each of the three authors referred to in the previous paragraph considers that social class is a major factor affecting racism. Thus, racism tends to take somewhat different forms and serve different functions among the upper, middle and working classes.

Both the nineteenth century and, to a lesser extent, the contemporary entrepreneurial middle class, have sometimes drawn on neo-Darwinian notions of 'survival of the fittest' to legitimise (justify and 'make acceptable') their own advantage over and, in some cases, direct exploitation of, blacks. It is easy to see that upper- and entrepreneurial middle-class notions of racial superiority might blend rather easily together as, indeed the two classes themselves have done.

Marxist Philip Cohen suggests that historically the British upper class has justified its exploitation of blacks partly by reference to theories of superior breeding (its own) and the 'animal-like' nature of blacks who, because of their supposed 'sub-human' qualities, are considered, as it were, 'beyond the pale'. According to the dominant ideology thesis, working-class racism is largely the result of the wider transmission of upper-class racism. However, as we shall see below, Cohen explains working-class racism much more in terms of its members' immediate experience of immigrants.

Cohen does not deal with the more racially tolerant and liberal views expressed by some of the professional middle class. These views form a crucial bastion against racism (and, indeed, fascism) but, as Husband observes, they are seldom put to any hard test and, indeed, members of the liberal middle class can indirectly benefit from racism. For instance, products or services may cost less as a result of 'cheap black labour' or a white middle-class person may be offered a house by a racist estate agent at the expense of a black person who was ahead in the queue. Liberal 'tolerance' may not be ineffective in a society in which such racism routinely occurs, and specific anti-racist policies may be required.

Cohen's analysis of working-class racism is quite original. He points to many occasions when black and white working people have acted together to defend and improve their economic situation, but he also frankly confronts the widespread racism among the working class. He explains it as follows:

> [T]he working class 'goes racist' when and wherever the presence of immigrants or ethnic minorities threatens to expose the ideological structures which it has erected to protect itself from recognising its real conditions of subordination. It is not because immigrants are actually undermining their standard of living, but because their entry into and across the local labour or housing markets signifies the fact that the working class does *not*, in fact, own or control jobs or neighbourhoods, that the immigrant presence is found intolerable.
>
> (Philip Cohen, 'Introduction: perspectives on the present', in P. Cohen and H. Bains (eds), *Multi-racist Britain*, Macmillan, 1988)

In other words, the illusion that they – the working people – 'own their own territory' is exploded by the arrival of 'rival' occupants, and conflict follows. As far as Cohen is concerned, the white working-class people who react in this way have mistaken the cause of their problems, which is the functioning of the capitalist economic system. Simply, it is capitalists, not immigrants, who have deprived working-class people of their 'territory'.

Figure 3.2
In *The Logic of Racism*, Ellis Cashmore studied four housing areas in the West Midlands:

Area		Type of housing
Newtown	(inner city)	Council estate
Chelmsley Wood	(outer city)	Council estate
Solihull	(inner city suburban)	Private
Edgbaston	(outer city suburban)	Private

Cashmore illustrates a varied 'pattern to racism: and class, age, and geographical location figure in the weave of this pattern'. These three strands are briefly illustrated below.

In the two council estates adults in both areas tended to see blacks as *competitors* for scarce resources, especially housing. However, among the young there was a difference in attitude. The white youth of inner-city Newtown were less likely to be racist because they sometimes appreciate that they share several problems experienced by black youth, including possible unemployment or low-paid, boring work. On the other hand, the outer-city youth of Chelmsley Wood, lacking 'personal contact and relying on second-hand knowledge and stereotypes for information', were more likely to feel 'a strong and crude racism'.

Among the middle class of Edgbaston and Solihull, Cashmore picks out three 'dominant themes' underpinning racial attitudes:

1 an opposition to state compulsion to prevent discrimination;
2 a need for ethnic minorities to assimilate to white cultural patterns; and
3 a stress on individual potential and application as the way forward.

Cashmore explains an interesting difference between the young whites in the two areas. In Edgbaston there is a small black population, mainly Asian; in Solihull, virtually none at all. However, the Solihull youth have a fuller impression of the complexity and variety of black minority life whereas, simplistically generalising from their own experience, those of Edgbaston tend to think that black youth should 'try to fit in' to 'our' way of life.

Although Weberians regard racial exploitation as distinct from class exploitation and as often occurring independently of it, they too link issues of race not only with those of class but also with other factors. The complexity of racism and its relationship with other factors is well illustrated by Ellis Cashmore, who introduces age and geographical, as well as class, factors into his analysis of four West Midlands' housing areas (see Figure 3.2).

Racism and racial tolerance: the fuller picture

Much of this book focuses on racism, not only because of the great damage it does – particularly to black people – but because it distorts the whole pattern of life in Britain. Widespread racism makes it impossible sufficiently to achieve the ideals of tolerance, justice and freedom which also exist in Britain. Very roughly, the evidence is that about a third of Britons are racist (about 19 per cent strongly so), a third neutral and a third tolerant. The two surveys illustrating these tendencies summarised in Table 3.2 below are a little dated, but more recent data on racist behaviour tend to support the finding that about a third of the population are racist (see Table 3.2).

Table 3.2   Percentage of sympathetic and unsympathetic feelings towards coloured immigrants (derived from Marsh, 1976, Table 1*) compared with the results of the work by Bagley (1970, p. 21**)

	Very hostile (%)	Hostile (%)	Unsym-pathetic (%)	Neutral (%)	Sym-pathetic (%)	Positive (%)	Very positive (%)
MARSH	12	13	17	25	20	10	3
	'Intense-outspoken'		'In the middle range'			'Tolerant'	
BAGLEY	14.2		52			33.7	

*A. Marsh, 'Who hates blacks', *New Society*, 37, 1976
**C. Bagley and G. K. Verma, *Racial Prejudice: the Individual and Society*, Saxon House, 1979.

Source: The Open University, E354, Block 2, Unit 5

It is possible to milk the above data to support either optimistic or pessimistic views about race relations in Britain. Indeed, as we move through the 1990s, it is probably true that Britain could either become a successful multiracial and multi-ethnic society or very much the opposite.

4 Racial and ethnic (minority) stratification

This chapter is divided into three sections. The first briefly defines ethnic/racial minority stratification and then examines links between it and class, gender and age stratification. The second introduces several interpretations of minority stratification in Britain: assimilationist and pluralist; underclass (John Rex); and Marxist. The third section discusses these interpretations in relation to employment and housing.

Undoubtedly a key issue in ethnic/racial stratification is the extent of upward social mobility among minorities. In turn, this is greatly affected by education. This issue is discussed in Chapter 5.

The relationship between minority and other forms of stratification

To stratify is to divide individuals into unequal categories on the basis of some difference or differences between them. Major forms of stratification are based on differences of class, sex, age and 'race'/ethnicity. There is no need to repeat here the earlier discussion of the meaning of the terms 'racial' group and ethnic group (see pages 3–6). The term 'minority group' will be considered to refer to both, or a compound reference such as 'ethnic/racial group' will generally be used. Only where a clear emphasis on culture (ethnicity) or 'race' is made will the terms be used separately.

Minority differentiation need not lead to stratification and inequality. In the United States, there is relatively little inequality between certain groups – for instance, the Irish, Italians and Germans. 'Different but equal' in terms of culture and rights is roughly the liberal-pluralist ideal – and the United States is perhaps the prototype liberal society. However, the Spanish and Afro-Caribbean minorities in the United States have not yet achieved equal status and this reflects deeper economic inequalities.

Britain remains highly differentiated in terms of some of its minorities, particularly those of Asian and African extraction. Again, difference and variety can be perceived positively. There are few Britons who have not benefited in some way from what minority cultures have to offer. However, members of Britain's black minorities disproportionately experience negative differentiation, with the result that their members are more likely than most others to occupy lower positions in stratification hierarchies (including those based on race, class or gender). How and why this happens in relation specifically to employment and housing is discussed later in this chapter.

Minorities and class

We have already discussed relationships between class and race/ethnicity and noted an important debate between Marxists and John Rex on the matter. In Chapter 3, the focus was mainly on international aspects of immigration – particularly the demand and supply of labour. The occupations taken up by black immigrants to post-war Britain have clearly structured their lives. The majority of black immigrants were and remain working class and, as a group, are more likely to be unemployed or low-paid than whites. However, there are significantly more middle-class black people of Asian than of Afro-Caribbean origin, and although this group is small, it is growing. The complexity of matters is demonstrated by the fact that some of the greatest poverty and inequality among black people is also experienced by people of Asian extraction: Pakistanis and Bangladeshis. An important point to consider in relation to black employees is whether their interests are best served by acting collectively with white employees – for instance, in trade unions – or whether some separate form of black or ethnic organisation is appropriate.

Minorities and gender

We now turn to consider the position of black women in the overall system of stratification. The sociology of black women cannot easily be divided into 'perspectives', but two general orientations seem to occur. Those who hold to the first consider that the position of black women is essentially similar to that of white women and that feminist (in some cases, socialist-feminist) analysis can account for and explain both their situations. Sheila Allen (see Reading 3, page 128) sympathises with this view partly on the grounds that in the important area of paid work both black and white women experience *comparable* levels of low pay and status. She therefore suggests that gender rather than race may be the effective variable. A second orientation gives much more emphasis to the distinctive position and disadvantages experienced by black women. An influential book which made this emphasis was Beverley Bryan, Stella Dadzie and Suzanne Scafe's *Heart of the Race: Black Women's Lives in Britain* (Virago, 1985), in which they argue that 'if you're a black woman you've got to begin with race'. They invoke a wide range of examples to illustrate their point, including offensive sexual stereotyping of black women and the relatively high rate of imprisonment among black women.

Hazel Carby's 'White woman listen! Black feminism and the boundaries of sisterhood', published in the collection *The Empire Strikes Back* (Centre for Contemporary Cultural Studies, Hutchinson, 1982) attempts to analyse the interconnections between class, gender and race within a broadly Marxist framework. She argues that the situation of black women in Britain bears comparison to that of women in colonised societies. First, in both situations women are in demand as paid labour, and, second, there has been a substantial effect on women's social and, particularly, family lives by the pressures put upon them by the capitalist system (whether in the Third World or in Britain). In the colonial context, the use (and often extreme abuse) of female paid labour frequently disrupted both their domestic work and work in their own wider economy and community. Similarly, in Britain employers have been more inclined to view black than white woman as 'normally' in paid work. This is partly, as Carby points out, because black women were initially encouraged to come to Britain largely to do paid work (albeit, mainly low-paid) and, one might add, because once in Britain many black women have *had* to do paid work to survive. So, while it can be argued that black and white women are part of the reserve pool of labour, black women occupy a distinct and particularly disadvantageous position within it.

Carby's discussion of black female labour causes her to deal with the controversial issue of the Afro-Caribbean family which, as we shall see, has an important bearing on the position of black women within the system of stratification. She and many other black writers object to what they see as characterisations of the black family as 'pathological'; that is, socially deviant and functionally inadequate. The basis of such characterisations is mainly that in the United States and Britain the number of single-parent families is much higher among females of African origin than among the white population. In Britain the number of children living in female-headed households is, respectively, 31 per cent for black women of Afro-Caribbean origin, 5 per cent for black women of Asian origin and 10 per cent for white women (figures, Policy Studies Institute Survey, 1984). A causal connection is made between black (Afro-Caribbean) single-parent families and high rates of crime and other forms of deviancy among young blacks, and high rates of dependency on social security among black adults (particularly females). A sociologist who has been among the most recent to make this analysis is the former American government adviser, Charles Murray. He argues that, because of the above factors, black people, and especially females, make up a disproportionate part of the new, dependent underclass in both the United States and Britain.

Carby refutes the pathologising of the black family by putting the matter in historical context. She points out that family, kinship and female networking (cooperation) patterns that worked well in Africa were often grossly disrupted by the impact of colonialism. These patterns were often extended rather than nuclear but, then, as she points out, the Western nuclear family is currently fraught with problems of its own (and, therefore, hardly a strong model to recommend). She further argues that in certain parts of the Third World women have had more power than in the West. Carby does not make great play of the impact of slavery on Afro-Caribbean family life but it must have been substantial and traumatic, particularly, in undermining the stable contribution of males. Carby seems to imply that the tendency of females to network around the needs of children was, almost as a matter of necessity, reinforced by disruption to family and kinship structures.

In discussing the Afro-Caribbean family in Britain, Carby again draws parallels with the colonial experience. She refers rather briefly to the frequent marginalisation of adult males in Afro-Caribbean family life and poses the issue largely in terms of the role of women: 'How then can we account for situations in which black women may be heads of households, or where, because of an economic system which structures high black male unemployment, they are not financially dependent upon a black man?' She stresses the enormous dual pressure on many Afro-Caribbean women as head of household and paid workers (they 'were encouraged and chose to come to England precisely to work'). Given such difficult practical circumstances, it is ludicrous to analyse the black family in pathological terms (instead, one might suggest an increase in wage rates for low-paid work and the establishment of an adequate national system of pre-schooling). In the absence of constructive help, it is not surprising that many black women appear to help themselves in the form of networking – although this is not to underestimate the loneliness and difficulties single parenthood can bring.

As Carby claims, her analysis of the position of black women in Britain questions 'the application of the concepts of "the family" and "patriarchy", [and] "reproduction"'. It will be clear by now that simplistic notions of 'the family' based on ethnocentric Western experience cannot be imposed on other cultures. Similarly, the patriarchal character of black male–female relations reflects family, economic and cultural differences compared to white people and so will take different forms. For instance, black women tend to be less economically dependent on black men than are white women on white men.

Carby is brief on the matter of 'reproduction', but she points out that black women have done substantial domestic labour in the servicing of white families. Overall, Carby more than establishes that the experience of black women has not been adequately addressed and theorised in the feminist movement and she herself goes some way to suggesting the issues which require to be confronted.

Minorities and age

Age and generation are particularly important aspects of stratification for recent immigrant groups. There are two reasons for this: one, demographic; the other, cultural. The age structure of groups of Asian and Afro-Caribbean origin is still weighted towards the young and middle-aged and contains relatively few persons over 65 compared to whites. This is because it was mainly young adults and their children who migrated some 30 years ago. Partly because of their sheer numbers, then, young blacks are more likely to be prominent in certain areas of activity, such as education and crime, than other age groups. Thus, because of its age structure, the black population is particularly 'visible'. However, this difference is likely to be negligible shortly, and to remain so in the next century.

A major consequence of the demographic structure of black immigrant groups is that relatively large numbers of young black people became unemployed during the late 1970s and eighties when unemployment generally went to very high levels. Other factors, such as racial discrimination in the job market and poor qualifications, also increased unemployment among black youth. However, the general increase in unemployment, including among black youth, was owing to large-scale economic circumstances. It was a period when, in Marxist terms, much of 'the reserve army of labour' was not being fully utilised. Undoubtedly young black people were 'blamed' by some of the press and public for being unemployed. This was bitterly resented among black youth. It is in this context that the urban disorders of 1980, 1981 and 1985 should be understood.

The second reason relates to the different cultural experiences of first and subsequent generations of 'immigrants'. For instance, students of Asian origin educated in the British education system gain experience – formal and informal – not open to their parents, many of whom will have been brought up in much more traditional, religious cultures. Although British-Asian writers consistently warn against assuming that this *must* cause widespread generational conflict within Asian families and communities, individual cases of friction do occur.

Interpretations of minority stratification in Britain

The importance of minority stratification is that it indicates whether and how minorities are achieving an equal stake with others in British life. Here we concentrate mainly on the Asian and Afro-Caribbean minorities.

The approaches presented below have all been discussed before in this book in different contexts. Assimilationist and pluralist approaches are grouped together here because, despite the differences between them, both regard it as a normal and natural development that minority groups will become part of 'the British way of life'.

By contrast, underclass theory argues that racism may prevent such development and create instead a black underclass. Marxist analysis also emphasises obstacles experienced by many black people but puts them in the context of class theory.

Assimilationist and pluralist approaches

Both assimilationist and pluralist approaches anticipate that the pattern of black stratification in Britain will eventually become broadly similar to that of white stratification and to that extent will be absorbed into the overall pattern of stratification.

The assimilationist approach assumes that 'they' (immigrants) should become like 'us', their hosts, who already own and occupy the country. Part of 'becoming like us' involves hard work and effort so that some immigrants will achieve upward social mobility and become middle class. Few now adopt this approach in simplistic form, largely because it is generally accepted that cultural differences between groups will persist. However, conservatives, such as philosopher Roger Scruton and educationist Ray Honeyford, argue that such differences should be relegated to the private area of life – family and community – and should not impinge on public areas such as law and social and educational policy. In these public areas, the same rules and practices should apply to all. Their expectation, then, is that minority groups should attain the same level of public conformity as others.

Pluralists differ from assimilationists in two main ways. First, they consider that ethnic diversity should have scope for public as well as private expression. Thus, they believe in a strong multicultural element to education (pages 70–2). Second, liberal pluralists have increasingly come to the view that black minorities will not achieve equality of opportunity in Britain without some state intervention (such as passing anti-discrimination laws – see pages 93–7). To this extent, they accept the analysis of underclass theorists, that racism in Britain is a significant obstacle to integration and racial equality.

Underclass theory (dual labour market)

Underclass theory argues that a black underclass is developing in Britain due mainly to racial discrimination. John Rex is the foremost exponent of underclass theory. The black underclass is largely lower working class or below the working class, and generally its members are in a worse position than most white working-class people because of racism. Douglas Glasgow has also used the term 'black underclass' to describe how a large proportion of the black population in the United States is stratified (*The Black Underclass*, Vintage Books, 1981). Glasgow particularly emphasises the low levels of upward social mobility out of the underclass caused by racism. In turn, this means that underclass status tends to become inter-generational as new generations are unable to break out of deprivation. A summary of the main aspects of underclass theory drawing on Rex and Glasgow is given in Figure 4.1.

Rex's analysis of the black underclass is based on Weber's concept of status distinction; namely, the allocation of prestige/position on the basis of a given difference. In this case, the distinction is made on grounds of 'race', especially colour. Thus, the black underclass is somewhat like a caste; that is, it is prevented from upward social mobility by inherited characteristics. However, Rex fully recognises that some blacks do achieve upward mobility so that caste parallel is only partial. Nevertheless, he further maintains the notion of caste by suggesting that the black class system and social mobility within it exist largely apart from

Figure 4.1   **Main points about the black underclass**
1 The main cause of the black underclass is racism.
2 Lack of upward social mobility is a key characteristic of the black underclass.
3 Because of the low rate of upward mobility, the underclass tends to be inter-generational.
4 Racism puts the black underclass in a distinct and different situation from the white working class (some of whom are racist towards blacks), creating a *dual labour market* (see pages 52–3).
5 Black people tend to lack *effective* connections with key institutions such as trade unions and political parties.
6 Black people have developed some of their own ethnic self-help institutions in all spheres of life.
7 Economic recession and restructuring (change) have worsened the position of the black underclass.

the white class system – a view sharply rebutted by his Marxist critics.

The concept of underclass has become widely used both in sociology and more generally. A more right-wing usage of the term 'black underclass' by Charles Murray should be noted. Whereas Rex concentrates on the economic exploitation and racism which he sees as structuring the black underclass, Murray focuses on what he regards as its cultural deficiencies, which he encapsulates in the term 'culture of dependency'. Finally, the term 'underclass', without the adjective 'black', is frequently used to describe all those cut off from the 'prosperity' and the means to achieve it enjoyed by the majority. Rex recognises the existence of such a larger group but contends that the black underclass, although part of the wider underclass, experiences particular disadvantage due to racism.

Marxist theory (reserve army of labour)

Marxists argue that in capitalist society, racial stratification must be put in the context of class stratification and related to the way the capitalist system operates. For Marxists, the social identity of all people, whether black or white, is primarily defined by the work they do (that is, their relationship to the means of production). On this basis, most black people in Britain are working class. However, it is an important part of Marxist analysis that minority groups are divided by class and that this occurs differently with different groups. Thus, Robert Miles points out that there are significant differences between the Asian and Afro-Caribbean minorities and that within the former group a modest number (such as some African Asians) already belonged to the wealthy middle class on their arrival in Britain. Marxists, then, counsel against sweeping generalisations about black people based on supposed racial or ethnic criteria.

There are now several significantly different strands of Marxist analysis addressing the issue of how analytically to integrate class and racial stratification. These approaches are summarised in Figure 4.2. The class/race model and migrant labour model both emphasise the primacy of class over 'racial' stratification and have already been fully explained elsewhere (see pages 16–18 and 21–3). Models (b) and (c) both allow that racism may occur independently of class conflict in capitalist society but differ in the extent

Figure 4.2 **Marxist perspectives on race and class**
John Solomos usefully summarises Marxist perspectives on race and class in his article 'Varieties of Marxist conceptions of "race", class and the state: a critical analysis' (John Rex and David Mason, eds, *Theories of Race and Ethnic Relations*, CUP, 1986). He distinguishes four approaches: the class/race model; the relative autonomy model; the autonomy model; and the migrant labour model. All four seek to explain the relationship between race and class.

(a) Class/race model
In this model 'race' is seen as a false concept which serves to distract attention from the realities of class to which both black and white workers should be addressing themselves. Solomos associates this approach with Oliver Cox (1948), and more recently with A. Sivanandan (1982).

(b) Relative autonomy model
This model allows that racism and responses to it have a limited independence (relatively autonomy) from class issues but that ultimately ('in the final instance') class/economic interests are more fundamental than those of race. Solomos considers *The Empire Strikes Back*, by Stuart Hall *et al.* (Hutchinson, 1982) to be a seminal work of this kind.

(c) Autonomy model
This model suggests that racial conflict *may*, in given situations, exist independently of class conflict and in such situations may be more fundamental than it. Solomos attributes this view to Gabriel and Ben Tovin. It is worth commenting that this view of racism seems little different than that often expressed by the Weberian John Rex.

(d) Migrant labour model
This approach largely reiterates that presented in model (a) but contextualises class/'race' relations in terms of the use and 'abuse' of migrant labour which is described as part of the 'reserve army of labour' (see page 22). Again, racism is seen as ideology – tending to confuse class realities. Robert Miles, whose work has been extensively referred to here, is perhaps the best-known exponent of this approach.

to which this may be so. The concept of 'autonomy' was introduced by French sociologist Louis Althusser. It means that certain ideological processes – such as racism – can occur more or less independently of class conflict. Model (c), in allowing that racism may occur independently of class conflict in capitalist society, seems almost to stand outside any traditional framework of Marxist analysis.

Stratification in practice: testing the theories against the evidence – employment and housing

Which of the above theories of racial stratification best describe the experience of the black people in Britain? One way to try to answer this question is to test the theories against the experience of black people in major areas of social life such as employment, housing, education and the media. The assimilationist and pluralist approaches will be considered together here because the evidence supportive of these positions is the same in this context; namely, evidence that black people are achieving greater equality with whites. At this point, it is important to stress again that the phrase 'black people' covers a large number and variety of groups. Each group has experienced racism somewhat differently and its members will have developed their own, sometimes distinctive responses to it.

Employment

This section first presents some of the important facts about the distribution of blacks throughout the occupational hierarchy and then seeks to explain them. The facts show considerable black disadvantage in the area of employment/unemployment. Figure 4.3 compares the percentage of white, Afro-Caribbean and Asian employees of both sexes in *low-status* occupations for the years 1974 and 1982. A far smaller percentage of white males hold semi- and unskilled jobs than do Afro-Caribbean and Asian. White females are about twice as likely as white males to hold low-status jobs, but in 1982, they were still considerably less likely to do so than Afro-Caribbean and Asian women. The pattern of black disadvantage is just as strongly apparent in the area of unemployment, and, again, females are generally much more disadvantaged than males (see Figure 4.4).

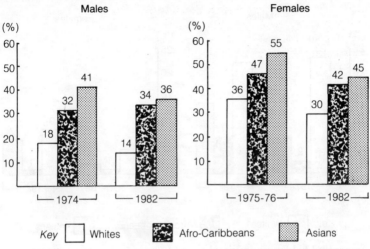

Figure 4.3   Low-status jobs: percentage of workers in semi- and un-skilled work

Source: 1982 PSI Survey (reprinted in *Social Studies Review*, March 1986)

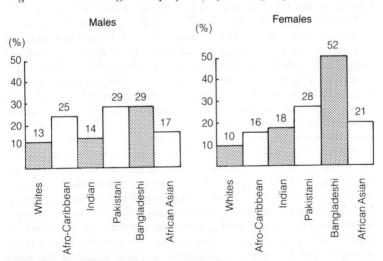

Figure 4.4   Percentage unemployment by ethnic group

Source: 1982 PSI Survey (reprinted in *Social Studies Review*, March 1986)

Figure 4.5   High-status jobs: percentage of workers in professional and managerial work

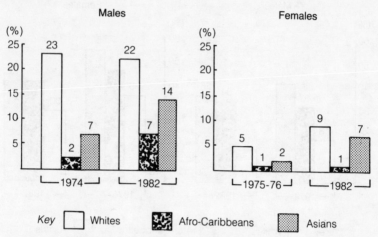

Source: 1982 PSI Survey (reprinted in *Social Studies Review*, March 1986)

Although a smaller percentage of all groups shown in the diagram were in low-status jobs in 1982 compared to earlier, the relative position between them had changed little.

There is a more marked trend towards racial equality in high-status professional and managerial jobs (see Figure 4.5) than in low-status ones – although white males are still in a position of considerable advantage. Further, Afro-Caribbean women have not participated at all in the trend to greater equality experienced by other black groups shown in the histogram. However, the percentage increase in other black groups employed in high-status jobs is significant even though far higher percentages of blacks are unemployed or in low-status and low-paid occupations.

We now interpret racial trends in employment in the light of the three perspectives outlined earlier. Evidence in support of assimilationist/pluralist approaches is mixed. There has been some upward mobility of black minorities into higher-status positions, but the majority of blacks are relatively no better off in relation to whites than were their parents or grandparents. Indeed, as Simon Field points out, the relative gap between the pay of those in high- and low-status occupations became wider in the early eighties and there are, of course, a disproportionate number of black people in the latter group. It is just such evidence that those who favour the black underclass thesis are prone to cite. The particular explanation given by underclass theorists for low pay and high unemployment among blacks is racial discrimination. John Rex, then, gives cause (racial discrimination) and effect (the formation of a black underclass in the system of stratification). Rex cites figures from his own research into employment in the Handsworth district of Birmingham which he considers support his argument that a black underclass has been created in Britain (see Figure 4.6).

Marxists interpret the same facts as Rex in a different way. Castles and Kosack (in *Immigrant Workers and Class Structure in Western Europe*, OUP, 1973) consider that most blacks are members not of an underclass but of the working class of which they form a 'bottom stratum'. Racism – of fellow white workers, as well as employers – divides them from the rest of the working class.

Writing more recently, Marxist Robert Miles takes more fully into consideration that significant minorities of some black ethnic groups are middle class. He refers to black groups within the working and middle classes as '*class fractions*'; that is, identifiable *parts* of these classes. He argues that black workers have been 'racialised', by which he means that their true class identity has been obscured by racism, including the racism of white workers. He expresses concern 'that the working class will be further fragmented if racism within the labour movement is not decisively curbed' (Miles, 1989).

Housing

Like the last section, this one proceeds by looking at the facts about race in relation to a given area and then examines the main interpretations of them. This section deals with the comparative quality of housing between black and white people and racial segregation in housing. Since the 1960s the position of Asians and Afro-Caribbeans in the housing market has improved considerably, as measured by certain key indicators such as the number of shared dwellings and the extent of overcrowding. This is in line with general trends. The percentage of Afro-Caribbeans and Asian households in shared dwellings fell from 48 per cent in 1961 to 5

Figure 4.6
Here, John Rex cites data on black employment and unemployment patterns of the kind he uses to support his analysis that a black underclass is developing in Britain (he cites housing residential patterns in a similar way). Yet Rex agrees that there is overlap between blacks and whites in various occupational categories. Partly, because of this, Marxists prefer to talk of a 'reserve pool of labour' containing blacks and whites, rather than of a black underclass.

The percentage of West Indians and Asians in our Handsworth sample who are in white-collar employment are 9.6 per cent and 5.1 per cent respectively as against 30 per cent whites. In a national sample, Smith found the figures for Asians to be slightly higher than this and for East African Asians to be higher still, but his figure for whites was 40 per cent. On the other hand, in our sample the percentage of West Indians and Asians in semi-skilled and unskilled work is 44.1 per cent and 38.7 per cent, and that of whites 27.4 per cent. Here Smith gives lower percentages for all groups except Pakistanis, but the gap between white and black workers is still wide.

In Handsworth it is fair to say that about half of the non-white population are employed in semi-skilled and unskilled manual work and less than 10 per cent in white-collar jobs, whereas only about a quarter of whites are in the low-skill groups and a third in white-collar jobs. That already suggests a considerable difference despite the overlap. If one then looks at industrial and occupational differences, one finds that the West Indian and Asian populations are more concentrated in labouring jobs and in hot and dirty industries, and are poorly represented in professional, scientific and administrative jobs. Both West Indian and Asian workers had to work extra hours to earn the same as white British workers, and were also more likely to be on shift work. According to Smith, unemployed rates amongst immigrants went down steadily in the years after immigration so long as employment levels were high, but rose relative to those of whites in times of higher unemployment. In 1976 we found that about 29 per cent of our immigrant samples and 13.5 per cent of our white British sample were unemployed and noted that although they formed under 10 per cent of the workforce in Birmingham, immigrant workers constituted 20 per cent of the unemployed.

These figures may not confirm that there is a completely dual labour market situation with whites gaining internal appointments and promotions in protected jobs and the immigrants getting what jobs they can in the open market. But they are consistent with the notion of two kinds of job situations with whites predominant in one and blacks in the other. In fact, the degree of apparent overlap may be deceptive and case studies of actual employment might well show that in each industrial, occupational, skill and social class category, the actual job situation of the black is less desirable and secure than that of the white.

(John Rex and Sally Tomlinson *et al.*, *Colonial Immigrants in a British City: a Class Analysis*, Routledge & Kegan Paul, 1979, p. 279)

per cent in 1982. The trend in overcrowding differs between Afro-Caribbeans and Asians. For the former the percentage of households with more than 1.5 persons per room fell from 40 in 1961 to 3 in 1982, whereas for the latter it actually rose from 1 to 12 per cent. However, the small rise among Asians in what is technically overcrowding *in small part* reflects a cultural preference for extended family residential patterns. On the other hand, the Bangladeshi and Pakistani communities are perhaps the poorest in Britain, and for some overcrowded accommodation is still all they can afford. Nevertheless, Simon Field's comments remains generally true: 'There is little doubt that the housing conditions of ethnic minorities have improved dramatically since that time [1961], both absolutely and relative to that of whites' ('Trends in Racial Inequality', *Social Studies Review*, 1(4), March 1986).

Field attributes this improvement largely to changing tenure patterns. There has been a major change in the tenure pattern of both Afro-Caribbeans and Asians although in a different direction. In 1961 only 3 per cent of Afro-Caribbeans lived in council rented accommodation, whereas in 1982 46 per cent did. For Asians, the increase has been in the area of owner-occupation, from 47 per cent in 1961 to 72 per cent in 1982 – the latter figure being higher than that for whites. As Field points out, despite the above trends, 'real inequalities' remain in housing conditions. A far smaller proportion of blacks own houses at or near 'the top end' of the market and more of them are at 'the bottom end'. Since Field made this analysis conditions at the bottom end of the housing market have notably deteriorated. In the mid and late eighties, the sharp increase in rents for council accommodation disproportionately affected Afro-Caribbeans, and again in the late eighties poorer Asian owner-occupiers were hit by very high mortgage interest repayment rates. Finally, the rise in homelessness in the late 1980s – partly due to the selling-off of council houses – particularly affected the poor and recent immigrant groups among whom blacks are disproportionately represented.

The extent of and trends in racial segregation in housing are an important indicator of the extent to which integration may be taking place in Britain. Both John Rex and Marxist urban sociologists agree that the majority of evidence supports the analysis that segregated cites have become a British norm. In her excellent book *The Politics of 'Race' and Residence* (Polity, 1989), Susan Smith reviews several case studies and census data and concludes 'that black people, immigrant or otherwise, are more segregated than the white population' and whilst segregation seems to occur less intensely than in some inner-city areas of the United States, it still occurs to a significant extent. Smith further points out that, whereas 43 per cent of Afro-Caribbean and 23 per cent of Asians live in the inner-city zones of London, Birmingham and Manchester, only 6 per cent of white people do.

Smith seems keen to narrow the gap between John Rex's Weberian-based analysis of housing segregation and inequality and Marxist perspective on the issue. Let us first describe Rex's position. As early as 1967, Rex and Robert Moore made a study of race and housing in the Sparkbrook district of Birmingham, titled *Race, Community and Conflict* (OUP, 1967). They argued that the differential access which individuals have to desirable housing divides them into *housing classes* and that partly because of racial discrimination black people tend to be in the most disadvantaged housing class. They saw the 'arena' of housing class-struggle as central to urban politics. Their own and more recent research finds that black people tend to be losing this struggle in so far as they tend to be concentrated in poorer housing in poorer areas – whether the housing is public or private. That this is still the case in the public sector goes against central government policy, which is that local authorities should seek to 'disperse' the black population. An 'official' reason sometimes given to explain continuing concentration is that black people tend to fall into certain 'administrative categories' (for example, one-parent families) which require specific housing. However, several pieces of research show that even when this is allowed for, differential allocation has occurred. Sometimes, however, black people may have been treated differently with good intentions. In the late 1970s, Tower Hamlets tried to deal quickly with problems of overcrowding and homelessness among Bangladeshis. However, in doing so, some were channelled into 'problem' estates, where housing was more available. Here they frequently became victims of severe racial harassment. More recently, the local authority has tried to place two generations of families close together and has been accused of racism for doing so. Clearly, public housing policy is racially a fraught and difficult area.

In the private sector, secret 'ring-fencing' (informal racial segregation) of 'white' areas and the funnelling of blacks into existing areas of occupation has occurred. However, this practice has been greatly reduced as Asians in some areas began to develop a semi-separate housing market with 'their own' estate agents, insurance agents and ethnic overseas banks.

Like other Marxists, Smith sees the relationship of black people to the labour market as more fundamental than their relationship to the housing market in explaining their position in the stratification system. Even so she shares considerable common ground with Rex. First, she describes the housing market as having a considerable degree of 'autonomy' in that access to housing can affect the labour market. Thus, racial discrimination in housing may prevent black people from moving to areas where jobs are more available. Second, Smith strongly agrees with Rex that black people have been disadvantaged in access to welfare, including public housing, partly through direct racism but also, indirectly, because central government has so underfunded inner urban local authorities that the needs of their inhabitants (disproportionately, black people) have been inadequately met.

The formidable argument and evidence of Rex and Smith make it difficult to mount a convincing case that assimilation is occurring to any significant extent in residential patterns. However, dispersal policies in public housing have had the effect of bringing about a slightly wider geographical spread among Afro-Caribbeans and there has been some 'suburbanisation' among an emerging Asian middle class. Some have suggested that black minority groups, like other cultural groups, 'prefer to live together'. This may, to some extent, be so, but it is most unlikely that they prefer to do so in inferior houses in environmentally inferior areas in which they experience deprived access to resources.

Conclusion

Arguably, the evidence presented in this chapter on how black people are stratified is inconclusive; that is, it can be used by advocates of all three interpretations we have been discussing. Underclass theorists and Marxists can point to substantial racism and class disadvantage experienced by black people and a continuation of segregated patterns of residence. On the other hand, improvements have occurred in the areas of employment which have affected a small but significant minority of black people and improvements in the quality of housing have affected the majority. Education is a further crucial area to consider in the stratification debate. If Britain is to provide equal opportunities to black people *in the long term*, then young blacks must be able to obtain fair and effective education in relation to other groups. If, on the other hand, they are discriminated against and poorly educated, then equality in the wider society is impossible. It is to the issue of education that we now turn.

5 Race and education

Education is always the hope of future generations. This is true in a special sense of immigrant groups. First-generation immigrants may accept and perhaps expect inconvenience and even prejudice but they invariably have high hopes for their children and grandchildren. Education is frequently seen as the gateway to a good job and a comfortable life for their offspring.

This chapter begins with a review of the levels of educational attainment of a number of ethnic groups in Britain. It then examines the explanations for variations between them in the levels attained. Finally, the chapter looks at several approaches to how the educational needs of ethnic groups can be met and problems dealt with.

A comparison of educational attainment of ethnic groups

As with the last chapter we will first establish relevant data and then seek to interpret it.

A problem with the data on ethnic educational achievement is that there is not a lot of it and much of it is not strictly comparable. For instance, on the question of comparability, some studies control for the class of the ethnic group compared (for example, compare working-class Afro-Caribbean children with working-class white children), whereas other studies do not.

Between 1960 and 1980, there tended to be a general consensus among researchers (and, indeed many teachers) that pupils from black minority groups, but particularly those of Afro-Caribbean origin, underachieved at school. In the 1980s, particularly the latter half, research has greatly qualified this picture in two ways. First, as more data have become available, it has become clear that there is a considerable variation in achievement *between* ethnic groups – some of it not anticipated. Second, as class and gender differences have increasingly been researched, variations *within* ethnic groups have become more apparent.

Table 5.1   Average performance of ethnic groups, 'O' level and CSE results, 1985

Ethnic group	Average performance scores of children	Number
African	16.9	426
African Asian	22.7	162
Arab	14.0	91
Bangladeshi	8.7	333
Caribbean	13.6	2,981
ESWI[1]	15.2	10,685
Greek	17.6	243
Indian	24.5	398
Pakistani	21.3	231
S.E. Asian	19.1	300
Turkish	11.9	268
Other	21.3	940
All	15.6	17,058

[1] English, Scottish, Welsh and Irish

Source: Adapted from F. Kysel, in *Education Research*, 30 (2), June 1988, pp. 83–9

Differences between the performance of ethnic groups are well shown in the research of Florisse Kysel into the 'O' level and CSE results in 1985 of pupils in the Inner London Education Authority. Table 5.1 compares the results of children from twelve groups (including 'other') in the form of an average performance score for each group. The performance score is computed by giving a certain number of points for each grade from 7 for an 'O' level 'A'/CSE 1 grade to 1 for CSE 5.

Perhaps the most striking point about Table 5.1 is the difference in the average performance scores of groups often classified by previous research as simply 'Asian'. Indeed, 'Asian' groups account for both the lowest (8.7, Bangladeshi) and the highest (24.5, Indian) on the table. Reasons for this probably include the more disadvantaged socio-economic conditions of Bangladeshis (that is, broadly, class factors) and the fact that they tend to have settled more recently in Britain and experience greater language and communication problems than most other minority groups. Similar points can be made about the Turkish minority, which has the second lowest score in the table (11.9).

Table 5.2   Comparative educational performance, 1976 and 1985

		Performance score	No. of pupils
Asian[1]	1976	18.4	389
	1985	18.9	1,124
Caribbean	1976	10.3	2,382
	1985	13.6	2,981
ESWI[2]	1976	14.0	19,820
	1985	15.2	10,685
Other[3]	1976	14.5	1,808
	1985	18.4	2,268
All	1976	13.7	24,398
	1985	15.6	17,058

[1] Includes African Asian, Bangladeshi, Indian and Pakistani pupils
[2] English, Scottish, Welsh and Irish
[3] Includes all groups other than Asian, Caribbean and ESWI, not just those labelled 'other' in Table 5.1

Source: Adapted from Kysel (1988)

It will be helpful to consider the performance of Caribbean children by 1985 by comparing it with the performance of this and other groups in 1976. Although the 1976 data shown in Table 5.2 are not as detailed as those given for 1985 in Table 5.1, they provide a useful basis for comparison.

In both 1976 and 1985 the score of the Caribbean children was the lowest of the groups shown in Table 5.2. This must give some basis for the concern about levels of attainment among Caribbean children. However, the improvement between the two dates in the Caribbean score was greater than that for Asians and the ESWI group (English, Scottish, Welsh and Irish).

To turn now to the second issue raised by current research: the growing awareness that class and gender factors greatly interact with ethnicity. The phrase 'interact with ethnicity' is important. For instance, gender factors seem to operate differently in Bangladeshi subculture (where girls generally underperform boys) than Afro-Caribbean (where in some circumstances, girls out-perform boys).

An early study which examined the relationship between class and ethnicity was Bagley's (C. Bagley and G. K. Verma, eds, *Race, Education and Identity*, Macmillan, 1979). The scope of Bagley's study was limited, but he found that *middle-class* children of Afro-Caribbean origin scored above the national norm on standardised tests. M. Rutter *et al.* (unpublished report to the DES, 1982), studying a wider socio-economic range of pupils, found that black students in 12 inner London schools were more likely to continue in education after the school-leaving age and *eventually* acquire more 'O' levels than white pupils. Later studies have confirmed this trend. When like is compared to like in class terms, therefore, ethnic groups tend to attain at levels much closer to those of white pupils. Further, the rate of improvement among most ethnic minority pupils is greater, including among Afro-Caribbeans, bringing them closer to the 'norm' for their class. For instance, in six Local Education Authorities studied by the DES *Committee of Enquiry into the Education of Ethnic Minority Pupils*, the percentage of Afro-Caribbean pupils obtaining five or more higher grades rose from 3 to 6 per cent and from 9 to 15 per cent in English language between 1979 and 1982.

Several studies report greater academic success among Afro-Caribbean females than males. Geoffrey Driver (in *New Society*, 17 January 1980) caused something of a stir when he published an article titled 'How West Indians do better at school – especially the girls'. However, the extent of his claim was limited to two schools in which Afro-Caribbean pupils, especially girls, obtained slightly more examination passes (at lower grades) than whites. Mary Fuller studied a more academic group in 1982, and found that, within it, Afro-Caribbean girls averaged 7.6 'O' level and CSE exam passes as against 5.6 for the black boys.

One reason given for the above pattern is that, although both black females and males often resent the education system, the former *use* it to achieve the qualifications they know they need to have any chance of success in the employment market. Fuller also suggests that academic success is one way the females can obtain a competitive edge over the males.

Despite the improving trend of examination results suggested in some of the above and other research, the educational under-achievement of Afro-Caribbean pupils continues to cause concern − not least, to parents. Sally Tomlinson usefully lists the explanations that have been offered for the underachievement of black children ('Ethnic minority achievement and equality of opportunity', University of Nottingham, 1986). However, she warns against attempts to find a single explanation for black underachievement and further comments that explanations 'lack a conceptual framework of understanding which factors, inside and outside the education system, affect the performance of these pupils in ways which are different from those factors which affect white pupils'.

Her list is used here simply as a convenient starting point for discussion.

1 *Intellectual capacity* Psychologists Jensen, in the United States, and Hans Eysenck, in Britain, have argued that black pupils as a group have lower innate intelligence than whites. There has been much scholarly criticism of this view. Recently, the Swann Report (*Education for All*, HMSO, 1985) on the education of children from minority groups reviewed the evidence in this debate. It dismissed the racial factor and concluded that 'ethnic differences in IQ scores are probably caused by the same factors as are responsible for differences in IQ in the white population as a whole'.

2 *Family structures and attributes* It has been argued that the one-parent family structure, particularly common among Afro-Caribbeans, tends to function to the disadvantage of the child. However, to regard the one-parent Afro-Caribbean family as merely disorganised and disadvantaged is to oversimplify. The black one-parent family is often embedded in a wider extended family-type system which acts as a self-help network. Where this operates effectively, it is possible that children experience certain advantages because they are socialised by a wider variety of adults (for further discussion of this issue, see pages 40–1).

Likewise, the view that Afro-Caribbean families are less interested in education than whites is also being sharply challenged, both by research data (Swann, 1985) and by Afro-Caribbean parents themselves (for instance, by the Black People's Progressive Association in Redbridge).

3 *Material disadvantage and socio-economic background* Class factors have already been discussed in relation to the educational achievement levels of black minorities (pages 59–60). They may very

well explain much about achievement levels but should not prevent examination of the possible contribution of racial/ethnic factors (including racism among members of the ethnic majority).

4 *Language* Communication can be a problem for those whose first language is not English (such as Bangladeshis) and for those who speak a dialect of English (for instance, many Afro-Caribbeans). It is obvious that provision must be made to enable the former group to learn and improve their English, and some local authorities have developed effective policies to do this.

The difficulties experienced by the second group have been less readily recognised. Teachers who treat dialect as simply 'incorrect' may confuse and unnecessarily demoralise pupils. Standard English is a form of English generally used in certain circumstances but, in itself, is neither better nor more correct than dialects. Pupils criticised for using their own dialects may be more inclined to reject school (see below). The dialect issue requires further research and, certainly, sensitive treatment.

5 *Self-esteem* In the 1960s and 1970s several pieces of research suggested that white racism often resulted in black children developing low self-esteem which, in turn, was seen as having a negative effect on their educational performance. Among the evidence cited for this view are a number of 'doll' studies in which black children tended to 'prefer' white to brown dolls. However, several critics have warned against drawing too clear conclusions from these studies. In addition, many black parents have rejected these negative images of their children. The good sense of this appears to be borne out in Anne Wilson's study, *Mixed Race Children, a Study of Identity* (Allen and Unwin 1987), which finds that mixed race children who are socialised to have a positive attitude either to being 'black' or being 'mixed' tend to develop a positive sense of their own identity. It seems reasonable to suggest that the same may be true of black children in general.

6 *Schools* The precise effects of schools and of teachers (point 7, below) on the attainment levels of black minority children are debated. In the early and middle 1980s, it tended to be asserted by general argument rather than precisely proved data that schools and teachers operated (usually unintentionally) so as to disadvantage, particularly, Afro-Caribbean, children. Thus Sally Tomlinson (1986) stated:

In particular, the ethnocentric nature of the curriculum, inappropriate curriculum materials, selection processes in school, particularly at secondary school option choice time, testing and examinations at all levels, and other school processes undoubtedly have effects on the educational performances of minority pupils.

Despite this emphatic comment, within three years Tomlinson was arguing on the basis of empirical research that schools which are good for white people tend to be 'about equally good for black people'. So, it is at least arguable that even if 'good' schools do discriminate against black pupils, this is somehow neutralised and does not prevent them performing up to expectation.

Recent statistical analysis also questions whether schools negatively affect black children's performance to any major degree. David Drew and John Gray in 'The black–white gap in exam achievement: a statistical critique of a decade's research' (Sheffield University, 1990) attempt to draw some general conclusions from existing research. Their complex analysis leads them to the following guarded summary, that:

> Schools certainly differ to some considerable extent in their effectiveness, but whether they are the major contributory factor [to Afro-Caribbean underachievement] remains unclear. To date we lack a study with a sufficient number of pupils and schools, covering a sufficient range of variables, with a nationally representative sample, combining both qualitative and quantitative forms of data-gathering to answer the question.
> (Drew and Gray, 1990)

7 *Teachers* A certain amount of intentional racism by teachers occurs, but it is likely that unintentional racism is the bigger problem. P. A. Green's study (University of Durham, 1982) of a sample of teachers and their pupils provides evidence that racially prejudiced teachers may behave in a discriminatory way against black pupils. Green studied 42 female and 28 male teachers who were all white British. The pupil sample consisted of 1,814 children – 940 white, 449 Asian and 425 Afro-Caribbean – between the ages of 8 and 13. Green first observed and recorded the interactions of the teachers with the pupils. He then asked them to complete an attitude inventory in which a prejudice scale had been 'hidden'. Twelve highly prejudiced teachers and 12 teachers who

scored low on prejudice were identified. The following is a summary of Green's findings (by Cohen and Manion):

Differences in the behaviour of ethnically highly tolerant and ethnically highly intolerant teachers:

1 Highly intolerant teachers gave significantly less time to *accepting the feelings* of children of West Indian origin.

2 Highly intolerant teachers gave only *minimal praise* to children of West Indian origin.

3 Highly intolerant teachers gave significantly *less attention to the ideas* contributed by children of West Indian origin.

4 Highly intolerant teachers used *direct teaching of individual* children significantly less with pupils of West Indian origin.

5 Highly intolerant teachers gave significantly more *authoritative directions* to children of West Indian origin.

6 Highly intolerant teachers gave significantly less time to children of West Indian origin to *initiate contribution to class discussions*.

Green's study usefully maps out broad areas of differential treatment towards certain ethnic-minority pupils. What is now required by way of complementing his quantitative approach is qualitative data on teacher–pupil interactions in multicultural classrooms, in particular the interpretations that each party places on the on-going dialogue or, as Green has shown, the lack of it in the case of certain ethnic-minority pupils and their teachers.

(L. Cohen and L. Manion, *Multicultural Classroom*, Croom Helm, 1983)

As Cohen and Manion say, the precise consequences of such intolerant behaviour by some teachers is not clear, but it seems likely to be disadvantageous to West Indian pupils.

It is not only in the behaviour of some individual teachers that unintentional racism occurs. Eggleston *et al.* (University of Keele, 1985) suggested that banding and streaming in the fourth and fifth years reflected teacher *expectations* of pupils as well as their actual achievement. As we shall discuss, racism among teachers should be understood in the context of racism in society. However, teachers do have particular power to help or hinder black pupils.

8 *Teacher training* It follows from the previous point that teachers need to be adequately prepared to teach in a multiracial society and that poor teacher training in this area might affect the prospects of black pupils. Issues relating to multicultural and anti-racist teaching are discussed later in this chapter.

9 *Racism, prejudice and discrimination* Several of the points already raised in this section indicate how racism in education might contribute to the underachievement of black children. However, racism in the wider society almost certainly contributes to the attitudes of some young blacks to education. For instance, racism among employers devalues the qualifications of black students who may come to believe that 'the system', including the educational system, is unfair and not worth their best effects. Such responses can contribute to the formation of anti-school subcultures (see Figure 5.1).

Conclusion

It is highly likely that any convincing theory seeking to explain the underachievement of Afro-Caribbean children will effectively relate several, if not all, of the above points. Individual or institutional racism in the educational system and, of course, in the wider society, inevitably affects the behaviour of black children. In contemporary Britain, relatively few young blacks appear to respond by losing 'self-esteem'. More common is rebellion of one kind or another. In general, girls and boys seem to rebel in different ways.

Although black girls may neither submit to nor especially respect 'the system', they seem more likely to try to get what they want from it, whereas black boys are more likely to form subcultures that are strongly anti-school. The quotation from M. Mac an Ghaill's *Young, Gifted and Black* shows how one group of young Afro-Caribbean males – the Rasta Heads – use language both to express their own solidarity and their rebellion against white authority. Yet, in doing so they are unavoidably sealing their own educational 'failure' – a price they seem willing to pay (see Figure 5.1).

Figure 5.1
One of the Rasta Heads' most creative and effective cultural practices was their use of Creole. In most lessons they continued their 'talks' in Creole, thereby using language as a mechanism of white exclusion. This was not simply a form of group argot. Their resistance to teacher strategies through language took various forms – for example, in the formal domain of the classroom, they frequently answered questions in mono-syllables. They were aware of the defensive attitude of teachers, and so they often challenged their authority by adopting the tongue of a defiant culture. Their language belongs to an oral tradition, which conflicted with the essentially written mode of the school. As pointed out in the last chapter, in their early years of schooling, Afro-Caribbeans are often viewed positively as possessing oral skills. The Rasta Heads' junior school reports detailed their high language competency. The teachers at Kilby school had not developed these skills. The Rasta Heads, aware that the official language of the school was a major instrument of their own deculturalization, had developed these skills in order to resist the teacher strategies.
   M. Mac an Ghaill, *Young, Gifted and Black* (OUP, 1988, pp. 104–5)

Educational policy: ethnicity and race

This section discusses the main approaches adopted within education to the increasing racial and ethnic diversity of Britain's population and particularly its educational population. The assimilationist, multicultural and anti-racist approaches are often seen as a trio of alternatives, although some argue that the last two are compatible. Table 5.3 summarises the three approaches in diagrammatic form.

Assimilation and education

Ethnic assimilation means that an ethnic group has become fully absorbed into the majority culture (see page 29). Whereas

Table 5.3   Education and race/ethnicity: three approaches – some key ideas

Assimilationist (Broadly conservative) A	Multicultural (Broadly liberal) B	Anti-racist (Broadly radical/Marxist) C
Immigrants came to Britain in the 1950s and 1960s because the laws on immigration were not strict enough.	Ethnic minorities came to Britain because they had a right to and because they wanted a better life.	Black people came to Britain, as to other countries, because their labour was required by the economy.
Immigrants should integrate as quickly as possible with the British way of life.	Ethnic minorities should be able to maintain their language and cultural heritage.	Black people have to defend themselves against racist laws and practices, and to struggle for racial justice.
There is some racial prejudice in Britain, but it's only human nature, and Britain is a much more tolerant place than most other countries.	There are some misguided individuals and extremist groups in Britain, but basically our society is just and democratic and provides equality.	Britain is a racist society and has been for several centuries. Racism is to do with power structures more than with the attitudes of individuals.
It is counter-productive to remove prejudice. You can't force people to like one another by bringing in laws and regulations.	Prejudice is based on ignorance and misunderstanding. It can be removed by personal contacts and the provision of information.	'Prejudice' is caused by, it is not the cause of, unjust structures and procedures. It can be removed only by dismantling these.
There should be provision of English as a second language in schools, but otherwise 'children are all children, we should	Schools should recognise and affirm ethnic minority children's background, culture and language, celebrate festivals,	Priorities in education are for there to be more black people in positions of power and influence – as heads, senior teachers,

Table 5.3   Continued

Assimilationist (Broadly conservative) A	Multicultural (Broadly liberal) B	Anti-racist (Broadly radical/Marxist) C
treat all children exactly the same' – it is wrong to notice or emphasise cultural or racial differences.	organise international evenings, use and teach mother tongues and community languages, teach about ethnic minority history, art, music, religion and literature.	governors, education officers, elected members; and to remove discrimination in the curriculum, classroom methods and school organisation; and to teach directly about equality and justice and against racism.

specific multicultural and anti-racist *movements* occur in education, this is not strictly true of assimilationism. In the 1950s and 1960s it was simply a widespread assumption that black immigrants would assimilate to British culture and society. The crudest version of this was that 'they' would eventually 'become civilised like us'. It was assumed that education would play a key part in socialising young blacks into 'the British way of life'. During this period, some local authorities wanted to avoid the development of schools with large concentrations of black pupils partly because this might prevent them from being sufficiently exposed to British influences. To avoid this, pupils were sometimes 'bused' to schools outside their own area of residence in order to achieve racial 'balance'.

In the 1980s, New Right (Conservative/Thatcherite) intellectuals adopted an approach to education which was implicitly and sometimes explicitly assimilationist. They argued that the educational system should support and promote what they saw as British values and institutions. All pupils within the public educational system should be educated in 'British culture' whilst ethnic cultures were largely left to private concern.

Roger Scruton, a New Right intellectual, argues that in Britain there is 'a common language, a dominant religion, a settled pattern of social expectations, a shared network of entertainment and sport, common morality and a common law' – the last of which he sees as part of common political culture. He contends that the prime purpose of education in Britain is to facilitate the participation of the individual in this culture and that 'there can be no real argument for a "multi-cultural" curriculum' (R. Scruton, 'The myth of cultural relativism', in F. Palmer, ed., *Anti-Racism – an Assault on Education and Value*, Sherwood Press, 1986).

Another prominent exponent of the assimilationist position is Ray Honeyford, who was a headmaster of a multicultural school in Bradford before his views led to his early retirement. Honeyford believes that education should meet the 'common needs of all children', and considers that multiculturalism tends to promote racial discord. At times, his writings are critical of black minority parents, particularly Afro-Caribbean, 'for lack of support for school and its values' (cited in Mark Halstead, *Education, Justice and Cultural Diversity*, Falmer Press, 1988).

Mark Halstead reviewed Honeyford's arguments in *Education, Justice and Cultural Diversity*, cited above. Although generally disagreeing with him, Halstead suggests that Honeyford was rather 'shouted down' (page 66) and gives his views careful consideration. Halstead's major criticism of Honeyford is that 'there can be injustice in treating people the same when in relevant respects they are different'. The sometimes deep cultural differences of children of Asian and Afro-Caribbean descent do not magically disappear at the school gate. Consideration within education must be given to these differences and to the racism they sometimes provoke even to achieve the situation of fair competition that Honeyford wants for all pupils. On the other hand, Halstead accepts that multiculturalists must effectively deal with the issue of common values and culture raised by both Scruton and Honeyford.

The National Curriculum made law by the 1988 Education Reform Act reflects, in milder form, the New Right view that education should promote national culture. For instance, Christian religious worship and religious education have been made compulsory – although there is provision for opting out of worship. At the time of writing it remains an open question whether, for instance, History and English Literature will be taught in a highly ethnocentric way or not, although the intention to assert 'national tradition' is apparent in the Act in respect to both subjects. The ethnocentric tendencies of the Act are, in some measure, balanced by the encouragement to schools to pursue multicultural, cross-curricular themes.

Multicultural education

Multicultural education is based on the view that education should fully reflect the ethnic *pluralism* of British society and develop an understanding and respect for the culture of others. However, multicultural education has become a broader movement than even this wide definition suggests. The Swann Report, *Education for All* (1985), gave official sanction to multicultural education but, in some respects, also endorses anti-racist education (see Figure 5.2).

The multicultural education movement began in the mid 1960s. According to Rob Jeffcoate, a supporter and theorist of the movement, it focused on several concerns. These were:

1 language: inadequate communication between teachers and black ethnic minority pupils; for instance, effective English as a Second Language teaching;
2 underachievement by children of Afro-Caribbean origin;
3 a broader curriculum – that is, a multicultural curriculum; for example, teaching materials should contain elements reflecting various cultures; and
4 the need to counter racial prejudice and discrimination.

According to Jeffcoate, in the 1970s the movement focused more sharply on the problem of racism. This was partly in response to a growth in assertiveness and relative popularity of the National Front. It is partly because the multicultural movement had developed a clear opposition to racism that Jeffcoate claims that multicultural education is quite capable of being effectively anti-racist. However, this approach is strongly opposed by the anti-racist theorist Chris Mullard, whose views are discussed below.

An important criticism of the multicultural education approach is that it concentrates on less important 'trimmings' – 'saris, somosas, and steel bands' – and fails to emphasise the essentials of education. In *The Education of the Black Child in Britain* (Fontana,

Figure 5.2 *Education for All: The Report of the Committee of Enquiry into the Education of Children from Ethnic Minority Groups*, **The Swann Report, 1985**

Education for All was the product of six years' deliberation. The Report argued that multicultural education is not only a right of ethnic minorities but also a necessity for the ethnic majority, whose ethnocentrism is a root cause of racism. In parts, the Report also argues that institutional racism must be removed from schools. However, critics have argued that it is not strong and consistent enough on this point and offers insufficient practical guidelines on how these goals can be achieved.

On the matter of policy, the Report quotes with approval the guidelines of the Inner London Education Authority, which are given below:

The policy

Each school or college will finally determine its policy in the light of its own circumstances. However, certain elements are common to all:

1 A clear, unambiguous statement of opposition to any form of racism or racist behaviour.
2 A firm expression of all pupils' or students' rights to the best possible education.
3 A clear indication of what is not acceptable and the procedures, including sanctions, to deal with any transgressions.
4 An explanation of the way in which the school or college intends to develop practices which both tackle racism and create educational opportunities which make for a cohesive society and a local school or college community in which diversity can flourish.
5 An outline of the measure by which development will be monitored and evaluated.

1981), Maureen Stone argues that the priority of black parents is that the educational system should meet the *educational needs of their children* – for example, provide sound skills in the three 'r's – rather than multicultural education which, in any case, might be incompetently handled by white teachers. Two surveys of the parents of Asian and Afro-Caribbean children, by Rex and Tomlinson (*Colonial Immigrants in a British City: a Class Analysis*, Routledge and Kegan Paul, 1979) and Smith and Tomlinson (*The School Effect: a Study of Multiracial Comprehensives*, Policy Studies Institute, 1989), tend to support Stone. They find that what most black parents want for their children in education is what most white parents want: teaching which enables their children to achieve high standards (see Figure 5.3). However, there is no reason in principle why education should not be both multicultural and of a high standard.

A main criticism of multicultural education from the political Right is that it is culturally relativistic, that is, it lacks a common core of values. In fact, the Swann Report, as well as advocating multicultural education, considers that education should also concern itself with values that are 'universally appropriate'. However, as Mark Halstead observes, the Report is rather vague about what these values are. He himself suggests the following as an absolute minimum framework of common values in a pluralist society: a basic social morality (as a framework for interaction); tolerance and a rejection of violence as a means of persuasion; an acceptance of a common system of law and government by all groups and commitment to seek to change these only through democratic means. Beyond this, he proposes that discourse in a pluralistic society must be *rational*. No group can claim a monopoly of truth but must open its beliefs to rational criticism just as it has the freedom so to criticise others.

As Halstead shrewdly observes, defined in the above way pluralistic education is likely to be less acceptable to Muslim fundamentalists than to Honeyford and the New Right (see pages 85–8). After all, there is a strong liberal strain – including a commitment to free speech – within the New Right which perhaps sits uncomfortably alongside its more prescriptive tendencies as expressed in parts of the National Curriculum.

Anti-racist education

Anti-racist education aims at opposing and removing racism not

Figure 5.3   Researchers from the Policy Studies Institute and the University of Lancaster spent seven years from 1981 following the progress of 3,000 pupils in 20 urban comprehensive schools from entry at 11 to public exams at 16. The percentage of ethnic minority children in the schools studied varied from 10 per cent to 90 per cent.

This is the first long-term study of its kind in the UK, according to Professor Sally Tomlinson, one of the authors of the report called *The School Effect: a Study of Multiracial Comprehensives*.

The children's attainment was assessed by tests on entry in maths, reading, writing and verbal and non-verbal skills, again after two years and on their exam results which they took in the year before the introduction of the GCSE. Researchers also studied option choices, and views of parents and children.

'If schools were improved only within the current range of performance of urban comprehensive schools this would be enough to transform the standards of secondary education.'

The study looked at the achievements of pupils from ethnic minority backgrounds and found that schools which are good for white people tend to be 'about equally good for black people'.

The report concludes that multicultural education should not be seen as a method of improving performance of racial minority groups, but as an aspect of good education for all pupils.

'The most important implication of the findings of this research project is that action is needed in the poorer schools. The measures that will most help the racial minorities are the same as those that will raise the standards of secondary education generally.'

Professor Tomlinson said: 'We hope the research will stimulate some deep thinking about a coherent overall policy for urban schools – not get-outs like CTCs which will be more divisive.'

From a review of *The School Effect: a Study of Multiracial Comprehensives*, by D. Smith and S. Tomlinson, PSI, 1989 (*Times Educational Supplement*, 30 June 1989, p. 10) merely within teaching and the curriculum but from *the structure* and practice of school and other educational institutions as a whole. This means removing racism from syllabuses and teaching resources; from the classroom; from appointments procedures; from the way management operates; and from wherever else in the educational system it may exist. Because anti-racist education is concerned with the purpose and functioning of the educational system as a whole, Chris Mullard, an influential exponent of it, has termed it a *structural* approach (as distinct from multicultural education, which he terms a *cultural* approach). Structural change means redistributing *power* in education to blacks and therefore reducing the power of whites.

Mullard suggests that there are three basic principles to anti-racist education: orientation, observation and opposition:

1 orientation means gaining a perspective on racism in British society and education – partly through discussing the matter with others;
2 observation means examining racism in schools and other educational institutions;
3 opposition means totally opposing racism wherever it is found.

The concept of structural racism can be developed partly in terms of institutional racism referred to previously (pages 8–9). Institutional racism can occur without individuals intending it to do so – sometimes because the rules or procedures of an institution are unintentionally racist. Thus, an interview panel with no black people on it might overlook the particular understanding and skills a black candidate might bring to a job in a racially mixed or all-white school. Mullard considers that if blacks are to gain more power in education, then more than 'equal competition' with whites is required. In addition, compensation for black disadvantage – past and present – is also needed.

Anti-racist educationists express concern about research, such as that of Smith and Tomlinson, which states that '[t]he measures that will most help the racial minorities are the same as those that will raise the standard of secondary education generally'. Anti-racists believe that, in addition to any general improvements in the educational system, what they see as the serious problem of racism within education must be diagnosed and dealt with.

However, anti-racists have recently begun to review their strategies for achieving racial equality. This is partly due to the comments of anti-racist practice made in the MacDonald Report which investigated the killing of an Asian schoolboy at Burnage High School, Manchester. The Report suggested that rigid and insensitive anti-racist policies may have actually worsened race relations in the school. In response, some anti-racists are stepping back from their own insistence on principle and instead educating themselves more thoroughly in the realities of minority cultures. As far as teachers and other public employees are concerned the intention is that better knowledge of minority clients should lead to better service for them. Although this trend is in an early phase, it seems compatible with a multicultural perspective and may herald a convergence of the two approaches.

Conclusion

In recent years, education has been at the heart of the struggle to redefine and regenerate British society. What kind of education we have partly determines what kind of adults our children will be and therefore what kind of society Britain will become. Behind the attempts to clarify educational purpose and direction perhaps lies a sense of national decline and loss of identity. There is as yet no consensus on the best educational means to release the energy and potential of the new multiracial and multi-ethnic Britain, but certainly there is no lack of passion and ideas.

6 Race and ethnicity: structure and culture

The opening section of this book cited John Rex's distinction between situations of racial conflict or cooperation and situations of ethnic conflict or cooperation (page 8). Whatever reservations there may be about his terminology, Rex's distinction is useful in differentiating between situations in which racial issues, particularly those involving racism, predominate, and those in which ethnic (cultural) issues are more apparent. An example of primarily an ethnic situation is the movement within several of the Soviet republics for greater national, cultural and political independence (see Figure 6.1). By contrast, the system of apartheid in South Africa reflects primarily racial rather than ethnic distinctions – however false these may actually be.

However, in reality, racial and ethnic factors are closely allied and tend to occur together – although one or other is likely to predominate. Thus, it would hardly be possible to separate the various racial and ethnic factors that have been a part of race/ethnic conflict in Britain during the post-war period. It is not easy to

Figure 6.1 Ethnic 'national' movements in the USSR

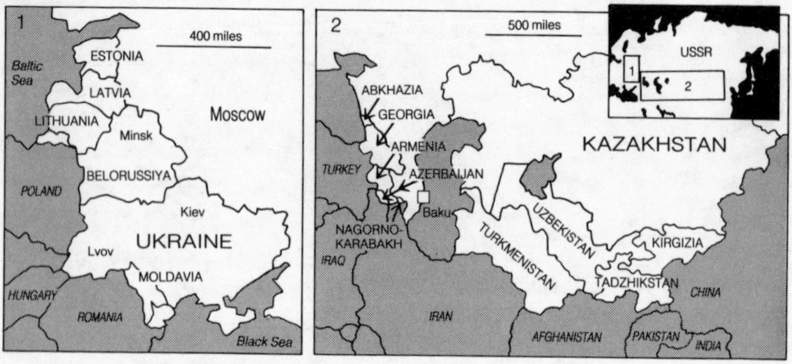

Source: Adapted from the *Guardian*, 1989

determine whether the familiar stock of popular stereotypical insults of Asians and of Afro-Caribbeans are based on racial or ethnic prejudice. Either way, the term 'racist' describes them.

We have already discussed the main theoretical models which seek to explain the process of minority cultural adjustment/ negotiation – assimilationist, pluralist and Marxist (pages 66–70, 70–2 and 72–5) – in the particular context of education. This chapter examines some realities of minority/majority cultural negotiation in relation to specific cultural fields. These include literature (briefly), the media and Blackpool Pleasure Beach (as an example of popular culture). The main focus of these sections is on evidence of racism in British culture, and the main interpretations cited reflect conflict perspective, mainly Marxist. There follows a section on black people's cultural responses to racism. The chapter then shifts in emphasis to discuss a major and celebrated example of ethnic or quasi-ethnic conflict: the Rushdie matter. It will be seen that ethnic conflict is not the same as racial conflict though racism can easily arise in ethnic conflict.

Racism in British culture: an overview

Research consistently shows that members of black ethnic groups are more likely to be the victims of racism than members of non-black groups (Political and Economic Planning, 1977 and Policy Studies Institute, 1984 surveys). The problem of white racism is particularly difficult to deal with as the trigger for it is often colour – something which is here to stay!

In this section, I propose to illustrate how pervasive racism has been and remains in British culture. It occurs both in 'high' culture, including academic life, and in popular culture. The following quotation from the *Encyclopaedia Britannica* of 1884 expresses an opinion common among the British elite over several centuries:

> No full-blooded Negro has ever been distinguished as a man of science, a poet, or an artist, and the fundamental equality claimed for him by ignorant philanthropists is belied by the whole history of the race throughout the historic period.

The reference to 'philanthropists' reminds us that there have always been some who have believed in 'the fundamental equality' of black and white people and that racial tolerance as well as intolerance is part of British culture.

There is no doubt that historically black people have often been presented in Western literature and the media as stereotypes. The important question is what effect such stereotypical presentation has had. First, however, let us look at some further examples of racial stereotypes from the vast number available. Two cases are provided by two world-famous English authors, Agatha Christie and Enid Blyton. The former titled one of her books *Ten Little Nigger Boys* – eventually it was retitled *Ten Little Indians* to remove the offensiveness of the original title. Enid Blyton's presentation of one of her characters, Sambo, would seem farcical were it not just one example of a wider pattern of cultural stereotyping. Sambo's owner, Matty, does not like him: 'I think you are ugly Sambo. . . . I don't like your black face.' Later, in return for a good deed, Sambo is turned white and receives this 'compliment': '"You've got the dearest, pinkest face that ever I saw!" Sambo could hardly believe his ears. He was a nice looking doll now as good as any other. . . . No wonder he's happy little pink Sambo.' A more straightforward assumption of cultural superiority would be difficult to find! It is probably fair to say that contemporary children's books tend to contain fewer stereotypical presentations of black people although many still present no black people at all!

The BBC itself has self-critically produced three films, *The Black and White Media Show* – 1, 2 and 3) in which clips of various stereotypical presentations of blacks are shown. These include presentations in which blacks are presented as 'a joke', 'stupid', and as in a highly subservient position in a social relationship. Significantly, Michael Grade, the controller of BBC 1, fully acknowledged that the presentation of race/ethnicity on BBC television was open to criticism. In addition to the need to remove any pattern of negative racial stereotyping, he thought more could be done to improve the presentation of ethnic culture and opinion. Such a level of awareness, at least, suggests a degree of commitment to non-racist and more culturally representative broadcasting, and it is arguable that both the BBC and ITV have recently made some progress in this direction.

Indeed, it is in the popular press that most racial stereotyping now appears to occur. Among the most aggressively insulting of recent examples are two front-page articles in *The Sun* about Asians attempting to visit or emigrate to Britain. The tone of the articles is well expressed in their headlines: 'The liars: whoppers Asians told at Heathrow' (16 October 1986) and 'Cheating Asians cost us £5000 a week' (27 November 1986).

Do such insulting and negative images have any effect or influence apart from the hurt to individuals and groups they must cause? Recent attempts to understand the effects of the media (particularly of portrayals of sex and violence) tend to reject simple cause–effect interpretations – for example, racism on television causes (some) people to be racist – in favour of more interactive models. Thus, members of the audience are seen as generally able to select and interpret media content rather than merely reacting predictably to it. However, individuals do not respond in a vacuum but within the context of their existing attitudes and values, which, of course, reflect those of the social groups to which they belong. Within this model, short-term exposure to media content on race would be seen as likely to *reinforce* existing rather than create new attitudes to race. Philip Elliot's research into audience response to a television series, *The Nature of Prejudice*, supports this analysis (*The Making of a Television Programme*, Constable, 1972). A hypothetical example can be used to illustrate the point: liberal intellectuals viewing a televised football match would be likely to find irritating or angering the baiting and booing of black players, whereas a member of the National Front might find it reassuring or amusing. Their responses to the headlines given in the previous paragraph might also differ along these lines.

To argue that short-term exposure to the media tends to reinforce rather than wholly create people's attitudes is not to underestimate its influence. Continuous reinforcement of a given attitude – say, a racist one – may strengthen it in an individual and probably increase the chance of others adopting it. Further, a survey by Hartmann and Husband on race in the media (*Racism and the Mass Media*, Davis Poynter, 1974) indicates that the media's influence may be more *general* than that of immediately stimulating the formation of given attitudes. They suggest that the media 'provide people with a picture of the world', parts of which may influence attitude development, particularly when people have no 'situationally based knowledge' (that is, first-hand knowledge) of a particular phenomenon. Thus, they found that respondents with little or no experience of blacks had broadly more negative impressions than those who had first-hand experience of them.

Hartmann and Husband explain this in terms of the tendency of the media, particularly the popular press, to present blacks negatively and in circumstances involving conflict.

Marxists, too, consider that the media present their audience with an influential picture of the world. In general, they argue that 'the picture' or ideology which mainly capitalist-owned media reproduces is favourable to the capitalist system. Such a summary statement, however, does not do justice to the detail of recent Marxist work in this area. In *Policing the Crisis* (Macmillan, 1978), Stuart Hall *et al.* examine the way the media presented 'muggings' as particularly a crime of black youth. They see this as a *scapegoating* of blacks which partly functions to direct public anger against them rather than against the controversial social and economic policies of the government. Marxists particularly see the unnecessary stirring up of racial divisions as a way of distracting from more fundamental problems of a non-racial character – such as why large numbers of both blacks and whites are in poverty. Thus, media-led 'moral panics', including those about race and 'black youth', tend to serve a reactionary function: the 'deviant' or 'different' group is stigmatised and condemned and the boundaries of 'normality' reasserted. This suits those who have a vested interest in 'the way things normally are' rather than those who have new claims to make. The wide scope of much Marxist analysis of the media is well illustrated in the collection of articles *Looking Beyond the Frame* (eds M. Reeves and J. Hammond, Links Publications, 1989). One contributor, Adrian Hart, points out how even well-meaning whites, such as those who run 'aid' organisations, often present blacks in a state of dependency on whites. Perhaps if there is one theme that runs through the many stereotypes of blacks – funny, cuddly, stupid, in need – it is that they are relatively *powerless* in relation to whites.

A case study

I will give an example from my own research on racism in popular culture which may demonstrate how deeply embedded and taken-for-granted racist assumptions are in British life. My area of research was the Pleasure Beach at Blackpool, and the occasion was a day in the summer of 1987.

The aim of my research was to note and photograph activities in the pleasure beach which featured race in any way. I found three. The first was an attraction called 'River caves'. Outside the caves was the depiction of a scene involving several life-size artificial figures. The scene appeared to be based on several well-known children's stories. Centre scene was Captain Hook manning the mast of a ship. To the right was a Robinson Crusoe-type figure shaking hands with a tall black person who was clad only in a pair of bright orange shorts, whom I took to be Man Friday. To the left of Captain Hook's ship were four black 'natives' carrying shields and spears and dressed similarly to 'Man Friday'.

The second 'amusement' featuring race which I noticed was called 'Cannibal Island'. The 'fun' in this attraction was to fire a jet of water at any of six targets, each of which, when hit, caused one of six artificial cannibals to act in a given way. These actions included 'swallowing' a bone; stabbing another cannibal; pulling a toilet-chain; and, in the case of the single female cannibal – who was bare-breasted – the effect of the water-jet was to make her head jump up and down. The targets – perhaps in unconscious symbolisation of British nationalism – were brightly circled in red, white and blue. In what was for me a moment of pathos, I watched a young black boy operate this obscenity of racism and sexism.

The third presentation of blacks at the Pleasure Beach was part of a boating attraction set in mock-up of Tom Sawyer's Mississippi. The two blacks who were part of the scene were dressed in brightly coloured shirts and trousers which had connecting 'bits' with over-the-shoulder straps. They faced each other in rather indolent posture.

It does not require a complicated semiotic analysis to appreciate the general message about blacks that these three 'amusements' convey (semiotics is the science of signs). Probably most negative stereotypes of Afro-Caribbeans that occur in British culture appeared in one form or another in these three 'amusements'. To make matters worse, they were presented in a particularly trashy and offensive way. Blacks appear as primitive and simple, and as suitable objects for ridicule, obscenity and aggression. In Cannibal Island, they are presented as very close to sub-human. No doubt this sort of imagery and amusement would cease to seem funny if a white person came across a series of images similarly insulting to whites in a Third World country.

There are many examples of such racism throughout British

Figure 6.2 **Patriotism and ethnocentrism**
It was mentioned previously that Marxists see an articulation (close relationship) between nationalism and racism (see page 28). Patriotism and racism can sometimes be similarly linked. What seems like patriotism to those who love their own country can seem like narrow ethnocentrism (favouritism towards one's own nation and bigotry towards other nations) to others. Not surprisingly, there are negative as well as positive images of the British both in the countries Britain has occupied and among the people who have emigrated to Britain. Here, for contrast, are extracts from a patriotic English song, from an Irish song and from an Afro-Caribbean poem critical of English oppression if not, precisely, racism.

Extract from a popular English song, 'Land of Hope and Glory':

Land of Hope and Glory, Mother of the Free
How shall we extol thee, who are born of thee?

Extract from a popular Irish song, 'If you ever go across the sea to Ireland':

The English came and tried to teach us their way
  and blamed us being what we are,
But they might as well go chasing after moonbeams,
  or light a penny candle from a star.

Extract from a 'Rasta' poem, 'Inglan is a bitch':

Inglan is a bitch
dere's no escapin' it
Inglan is a bitch
y'u bettah face up to it.

culture. They occur in comics, newspapers, radio and television, in sport, and in everyday relationships and activities. We now look at how blacks respond to the racism they experience.

Black people's cultural responses to racism

Racism has had a larger impact on the cultures of black groups than other ethnic groups in Britain, simply because they have been the greatest victims of it. Black responses to racism have been extremely varied. Here I will consider only the responses of Afro-Caribbeans to racism. At one extreme has been a powerless acceptance of white domination – of the 'Uncle Tom' stereotype; the other has been the revolutionary rejection of white supremacy and, in the case of some activists, of capitalism as well. More commonly perhaps, most blacks have learnt to 'deal with' a racist system whilst criticising it and, in some cases, seeking to change it.

There is some truth in the view that the black immigrants of the 1950s and 1960s 'gave Britain a chance' to treat them as equals whereas their children and grandchildren have become more angry and indignant at racism. The sharpest and most dramatic expression of this anger was what the press called the 'riots' and black activists more usually refer to as the 'uprisings' of 1981 and 1985. These explosions of rage occurred against a long-term background of frustration felt by many young blacks, especially Afro-Caribbeans. When alienated from school and 'shit work', young Afro-Caribbeans, in particular, have found identity and solidarity within the peer group. Frequently, commentators have stressed the conflicts black youths experience with 'authority' – teachers, the police, probation officers. Stuart Hall has described this life-style as 'cultural resistance' (see page 101 for a fuller account).

Many of these peer groups possess great cultural vitality and creativity. For instance, in terms of style, presentation and, often, meaning, the music of young black artistes has emerged as a dominant force in British pop, as well as jazz. As Simon Jones has shown in *Black Culture, White Youth* (Macmillan, 1989), the appeal of reggae extends to many white as well as black youths. Jones suggests that such shared experience is likely to have a favourable spin-off in terms of race relations.

Of course, the black community urgently seeks success for its youth in careers other than music. In part, the success of young blacks in music – and other areas of entertainment, including sport – is because they have been deflected from more conventional careers, partly by racism. Unless other avenues of achievement open more widely to young blacks, it is difficult to see how race relations in Britain can greatly improve.

Figure 6.3   **Class and cultural variety among Afro-Caribbeans**

There is vast variety *within* both Afro-Caribbean and Asian ethnic groups, and the cultural differences *between* them probably exceed those between Europeans. Below, a diagram is presented which attempts to make some broad links between class and culture (life-style) among the Afro-Caribbean community. It is freely adapted from Ken Pryce's analysis of black class/culture given in his book, *Endless Pressure* (Bristol Classical Press, 1986). The point here is to show that culture is not 'free-floating' but located in structural realities, including class.

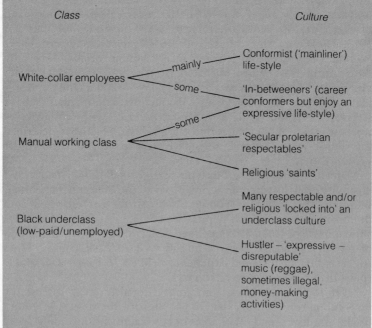

Relatively few Afro-Caribbeans have white-collar jobs. Pryce describes most of these as 'mainliners'; that is, as conforming, stable, law-abiding citizens. The same is true of the majority of the manual working class whom Pryce divides into religious ('saints') and non-religious – partly in recognition of the importance of religion in Afro-Caribbean culture. Some white-collar and manual employees enjoy an expressive (extrovert, pleasure-seeking) leisure life-style which may bring them into contact with the 'disreputable' life-style of the 'hustler' (criminal). Hustlers tend to be youths and young adults who, in some ways, are the most energetic and enterprising among an underclass whose members struggle to survive against racial and class disadvantage.

Salman Rushdie and Muslim Britain

Whereas the previous sections have dealt with racism and responses to it, this one deals with clashes between groups that occur as a result of specific differences of belief and principle. Such differences have helped to cause social chaos and great suffering in Northern Ireland, the Lebanon and elsewhere.

The publication of Salman Rushdie's *The Satanic Verses* and the subsequent *fatwa* (order of death) made upon him by the late Ayatollah Khomeini is of profound cultural significance as well as, of course, a personal tragedy for Rushdie. The importance of the continuing conflict around *The Satanic Verses* is that it has brought into sharp focus several key issues of ethnic relations in Britain. First, it has directed public and media attention towards a large section of Britain's Asian community – specifically, the one million plus who are Muslims. Previously, Asians have tended to attract less attention than Afro-Caribbeans and this has allowed mistaken impressions to develop. Second, the strongest initial reaction to the order of death against Rushdie among white Britons came from a group previously publicly well-disposed to Britain's black population – liberal intellectuals. Third, the crux of the matter is that the Rushdie conflict has raised the issue of ethnic cultural *incompatibility* in a way that cannot be avoided. The stark possibility is that certain cultural assumptions of Muslims may contradict those of the majority of Britons. In this case, the incompatibility is a conflict over two contradictory principles: the religious right and necessity to punish a blasphemer versus the right of an artist (and other citizens) to freedom of expression.

The latter is a core value of liberal, secular society. The following two quotations – the first from Ayatollah Khomeini's *fatwa* and the second from a response by the author Anthony Burgess – fully illustrate this collision of principle:

> I call on all zealous Muslims to execute them [Rushdie and his publishers] quickly, wherever they find them, so that no one will dare to insult the Islamic sanctions. Whoever is killed upon this path will be regarded as a martyr, God willing.
> (*Observer*, 19 February 1989)

> To order outraged sons of the prophet to kill him and the directors of Penguin Books on British soil is tantamount to a *jihad* (holy war). It is a declaration of war on citizens of a free country and as such it is a political act. It has to be countered by an equally forthright, if less murderous, declaration of defiance.
> (*Independent*, 15 February 1989)

It is essential to be scrupulously fair to the Muslim community at this point. Many – it may be an overwhelming majority – did not interpret the *fatwa* to mean that they should seek to break British law, and many have stated their intention of remaining within British law. However, some – who can be termed 'fundamentalists' – believe that 'divine' law should direct their conduct in society, including British society. Such a situation clearly has a potential for conflict far beyond the Rushdie matter.

Rushdie has not been short of liberal intellectual champions in addition to Burgess. Among these are the television presenter Michael Ignatieff, the author Fay Weldon and playwright Tony Harrison. To varying extents, their responses illustrate the three points made above. They all made their basic commitment of principle quite clear: they totally support Salman Rushdie's right to freedom of expression. However, unusually for liberals, two of them, Weldon and Harrison, raise worried questions about Muslim culture itself. Weldon feels that 'something has gone wrong' in relations between many white and Muslim Britons and that responsibility lies on both sides. In the past, Muslim communities have tended to 'get on with their own lives' in a rather self-contained way and lazily tolerant liberals have let them do so. The result seems to be mutual ignorance. Weldon appears to believe that a tough dialogue is now needed.

If toughness is needed, then, Tony Harrison's documentary drama *The Blasphemer's Banquet* certainly fitted the bill. The guests at Harrison's 'banquet' were Voltaire, Byron, Molière, Omar Khayyam and Salman Rushdie. These 'blasphemers' have his respect because they oppose what he sees as the intolerance of religious fundamentalism, of which he provides a series of examples in his programme. Harrison powerfully mixes images of religious fanaticism – from the grotesque hysteria which occurred at the Ayatollah Khomeini's funeral to book burning in Bradford. Don't burn books and don't threaten authors is his message – the Nazis did that . . .

Michael Ignatieff took the same stand in a programme in which he visited Bradford, a town with a large Muslim population, to explore the Rushdie conflict: like Harrison, he compared the totalitarianism of Khomeini so that of Hitler. In Ignatieff's words, Khomeini 'threatens everything'; namely, the values of liberal society to which Ignatieff is committed. However, Ignatieff was more puzzled than angered. He frankly admitted that he knew little or nothing about the Muslim community in Britain:

> I expected a community in a bell jar, sealed off from the rest of British society . . . and instead I found a community that is deeply, militantly British, down even to the Yorkshire accent. But I'm also finding the Rushdie affair has been a trauma for them, leading them to draw back from us, to defend a heritage they feel we don't understand.
>
> (Cited in the *Guardian*, 9 May 1989)

It may help in understanding the disturbing clash between liberalism and the Muslim religion if we further examine the origin of both ideologies. Although liberalism and religion are quite compatible, liberalism developed hand in glove with secularisation, the process by which societies come to be operated in accordance with non-religious rather than religious rules and procedures. Liberalism is part of secular ideology in that it argues that progress depends on the use of reason (including science) – regardless of religion. Broadly, these secular, religious beliefs have become the basis of principle or the ideology on which British and other Western societies operate.

In Muslim states a more traditional situation prevails. In Iran, Iraq, Pakistan and elsewhere, Islamic (Muslim) law is the basis of state law. The separation of civil and criminal from all religious law in Britain is not what many Muslim immigrants are used to. It is precisely this sensitive point that the Ayatollah's *fatwa* aggravated.

In the period since the *fatwa*, both uncompromising and more conciliatory moves have occurred. There has also been the unpredicted conversion of Rushdie to the Muslim faith and the tensions and complications of a war against a mainly Muslim country, Iraq. Britain cannot afford to alienate much of its Muslim community, and British Muslims cannot afford to alienate themselves from much of the rest of the nation, including its liberal intelligentsia (many of whom are sympathetic to the cause of racial/ethnic tolerance and equality). As far as one, apparently small, Muslim fundamentalist group, led by Dr Siddiqi of the Muslim Institute, is concerned, matters have become polarised to the point where he has talked of creating 'in Britain institutions normally associated with a sovereign territorial state'. However, other Muslim spokespersons, including Hesham el Essawy, director of the Islamic Society for Racial Tolerance, condemned such proposals as damaging to race relations and have stressed their loyalty to Britain. Liberals have continued to defend the principle of freedom of speech, but others besides Ignatieff have realised how little they know about British Muslims and have begun to educate themselves accordingly (see page 76). The view has also been expressed that authors might, at least, *consider* the feelings of religious people (as well as other groups) without impairing their own freedom of expression. It may be that such modest response to the matter offers more hope for future reconciliation than grandiose statements of principle.

Conclusion

The analysis and solutions to the problems of racism and ethnic conflict discussed here fall very broadly into the categories of culture and structure.

Those who adopt cultural solutions tend to take the view that socialisation is the key means by which racism and ethnocentrism can be attacked and attitudes and behaviour reflecting belief in racial equality established. Education is the agency of socialisation most accessible to policy-makers, and, as we have seen, there has been substantial effort in this area by both assimilationists and multiculturalists. The family is regarded as a highly private area, and nobody has suggested that government should try to *force* parents to socialise their children to be non-racist. However, considerable attention has been given to the socialising effect of the media – which greatly influences family members – in relation to race and ethnicity. As described earlier in this chapter, some attempts have been made to reduce racial stereotyping in the media and to widen the presentation of ethnic cultures, but critics argue that the popular press remains prone to both racism and ethnocentrism as, to perhaps a lesser extent, does popular broadcasting.

Those who adopt structural solutions to racism in Britain concentrate on trying to change the racist way in which institutions function. To be effective, cultural change must be related to structural change. Both neo-Weberian underclass theorists and Marxists consider that if black people are to achieve equality it is necessary that employment, housing, education and other major institutional areas of society operate in a non-racist way. They differ from one another somewhat in how this might be achieved. Underclass theorist John Rex believes that if the position of blacks in Britain is to be substantially improved it will largely be because of their own organisation and efforts. Alliances with whites must be made from a basis of ethnic strength. As far as culture is concerned, Rex welcomes the strong, positive images generated within black subculture since the sixties, and sees a continuing need to reject and discredit negative stereotypes. The latter process should complement the movement to improve material conditions.

Although Marxists may differ among themselves on the precise relationship between class and race/ethnicity, they agree that racial inequality, like class inequality, will only be fundamentally eradicated in a socialist society. Socialism is the structural change they ultimately seek, and racism will have no role in a socialist society. Of course, few socialists believe that socialism can be introduced 'overnight' and, as we have seen, Marxist analysis of how change might occur is often quite complex. Culture, of course, has an important part to play in virtually all Marxist models of change, but traditionally Marxists have been concerned that ethnic (and national) cultures should not divide working people from one another. They regard religious separatism and such nationalistic tendencies as the 'back to Africa' movement among Rastafarians with caution. For them ethnic consciousness needs to be informed by class consciousness otherwise it can become reactionary and escapist.

7 Racism, equality and the law

This chapter deals with four aspects of the law in relation to ethnic minority groups, in Britain. They are:

1 The law and immigration/nationality;
2 The law and discrimination;
3 Racial harassment; and
4 Crime and the Afro-Caribbean community: myth and reality.

The first two aspects, concerning immigration and discrimination, are closely connected. Together they represent the liberal compromise solution to race relations in Britain (see below). Various elements of this compromise have been in place for between 15 and 30 years and it is opportune to review their overall impact. The third aspect suggests that race relations policy has had little effect in reducing racial harassment and that immigration policy may even have made it worse. The fourth suggests that, however we interpret the complex matter of crime in the Afro-Caribbean community, analysis provokes pessimism rather than optimism about the quality of race relations in Britain.

The law and immigration/nationality

Immigration law and racial discrimination in Britain are closely linked, and so the division between this and the next section is one of convenience. First, some critics of British immigration law consider that certain features of it are racially discriminatory in themselves and also that it is frequently enforced in a racist way. Second, since 1962, it has in practice been the policy of both Conservative and Labour parties to reduce the immigration of black people into Britain whilst stating their opposition to racial discrimination in Britain. Because in part the anti-discrimination race-relations legislation was implemented as a 'trade-off' to compensate for increasingly tight immigration policy, it is useful to list the two together (see Figure 7.1).

Figure 7.1 **Immigration/nationality and race relations legislation: the 'liberal compromise'**

1948 *British Nationality Act*

Commonwealth citizens allowed freely to enter and settle in Britain.

1962
Commonwealth Immigrants Act
removed the rights of the 1948 Act for most New (black) Commonwealth citizens. Instead, a limited number of *employment vouchers* were issued.

1965
Race Relations Act
(i) made illegal discrimination in certain places, *but* the means of enforcing the Act were very weak. (ii) made incitement to racial hatred illegal.

1968
Commonwealth Immigrants Act
restricted the entry to East African Asians who held UK passports issued by the British government.

1968
Race Relations Act
enlarged the scope of the 1965 Act (discrimination being made illegal in employment and housing, for the first time) *but* enforcement still weak, relying on the new *Community Relations Council* to take up *individual complaints*.

1971
Immigration Act
made a distinction between patrials (those born in Britain or with a parent/grandparent born in Britain), who kept full British citizen's rights; and non-patrials (mainly black, New Commonwealth), who were required to obtain work permits prior to entry.

1976
Race Relations Act
extended the anti-discrimination laws to *unintended* as well as intended discrimination – a very important principle.

1981
British Nationality Act
Restricted forms of British
nationality provided for
those whose entry rights had
been removed by previous
laws – by this time the entry
of blacks for settlement is
highly controlled and
virtually limited to close
relatives.

1988
Immigration Act
An immigrant husband who
wants his wife and children
to join him in Britain has to
prove he can house and
support them.

The British Nationality Act 1948 enacted the rights of British citizenship to residents of all Commonwealth countries, regardless of the colour of their inhabitants. Citizens of the British Commonwealth could enter Britain freely, and work, settle and bring in their families. Both Labour and Conservative parties supported the Act. The reasons for passing the Act were both practical and idealistic: black immigration increased the labour supply but it also provided a concrete example of freedom and equality within the Commonwealth (see pages 31–3).

Since 1948, there has been a steady retreat from the ideals of the 1948 Act. As Figure 7.1 shows, the immigration of black people into Britain has been made more and more difficult. In addition, in 1981 a new British Nationality Act was passed which established several categories of British nationality and accompanying rights. The Act repeated a distinction first implemented in the 1971 Immigration Act. Right of abode in Britain was restricted to those either born in Britain or who had a parent or grandparent born in Britain. The latter category included millions of people living the mainly 'white' Commonwealth but very few people living in the mainly 'black' Commonwealth. This was what was intended. Both the Labour Party and the Liberal Democrats regard the 1971 Act as racially discriminatory.

Since 1971 very little primary immigration into Britain of people from the New Commonwealth and Pakistan (NCWP) has occurred. Primary immigration means immigration of people who do not already have close relatives settled in Britain. Most immigrants from the NCWP are immediate family members of people who have already migrated and who are British citizens. However, people from the NCWP attempting to rejoin their families have often found the process of immigration difficult and, in some cases, humiliating. For instance, brides-to-be, seeking to join their fiancés, have sometimes been subjected to virginity tests; male fiancés have to prove no 'prior purpose' (no other reason for wanting to immigrate than joining their fiancées) – a requirement which has excluded many males of Asian origin. Many parents – particularly single parents – have experienced great difficulty in enabling their children to immigrate into Britain because immigration officials have not been convinced of the parentage of the children. Even in those cases when genetic tests have established the identity of the children, delay has typically continued. Critics of government policy and of some immigration officials argue that the evidence is clear that the inconvenience and delay experienced by legitimate would-be black immigrants is intentional and racist. Even after immigration, black immigrants sometimes claim that they are victimised as a result of the negative climate fostered by the immigration legislation – for example, being told 'Show your passport' by suspicious officials. Further examples of what critics see as racist behaviour in the area of immigration enforcement are given in Figure 7.2.

The number of immigrants under the 1971 Immigration Act from the NCWP (mainly of blacks) has fallen steadily from about 75,000 in 1976 to about 21,000 in 1987, whereas immigration from elsewhere (mainly of whites) has remained roughly constant at about 25,000 a year.

The law and discrimination

The main Race Relations Acts passed since the mid 1960s have all been the work of Labour governments (whereas all the Immigration/Nationality Acts, with the exception of the 1968

Figure 7.2
In his pamphlet 'Citizenship for some: race and government policy: 1979–1989' (1989), Paul Gordon catalogues a variety of immigration policies which, taken together, he regards as 'state racism'. In addition to some mentioned in the main text here, his examples include: a sharp drop in the number of people granted refugee status in Britain (although the numbers granted the lesser security of temporary refuge has increased); an increase in the numbers of deportations (an Act passed in 1988 facilitated deportation and in 1989 deportations greatly increased); a rise in the numbers put in immigration detention which reached a new high of 11,000 in 1986 (detention is without trial and can be for 18 hours a day and without visiting rights); administration of immigration law sometimes in a way apparently aimed at delaying and inconveniencing black would-be immigrants.

Commonwealth Immigrants Act, have been passed by Conservative administrations). Originally, Labour had opposed the 1962 Commonwealth Immigrants Act which removed the automatic right of Commonwealth citizens to settle in Britain. However, when Labour came to power in 1964 it did not repeal the Act. Similarly, when it came to power in 1974 it did not repeal the even more restrictive 1971 Immigration Act.

Since 1964, Labour has pursued a two-pronged policy towards the legal framework for race relations. It has let stand immigration/nationality legislation which, in effect, has drastically reduced black immigration, and it has promoted a series of laws making racial discrimination illegal in major areas of British life. Roy Hattersley, among other Labour politicians, argued that, for the anti-discrimination legislation to be acceptable to the British public, black immigration had to be reduced. In so far as Labour has accepted Conservative immigration/nationality legislation and the Conservatives have accepted Labour race relations legislation, we can speak of a bi-partisan policy towards race/immigration. However, there is no doubt that the majority of the black community regard Labour as more sympathetically disposed to them than the Conservatives.

Figure 7.3 **Protection against racial discrimination provided by the 1976 Race Relations Act**

Employment: as a job applicant;
Housing: as a house-buyer; as a tenant or prospective tenant;
Education: as a school pupil, student or trainee;
Commerce: as a customer or client of any organisation or person concerned with the provision of goods, facilities or services;
Leisure: as a member or prospective member of a club.

The Act also provides protection against discrimination in many other circumstances.

Figure 7.1 summarises the main terms of the Race Relations Acts of 1965, 1968 and 1976. Because the Acts build on each other – racism and discrimination being increasingly made illegal – it is sufficient to consider only the 1976 Act in detail (Figure 7.3).

The Act makes both direct and indirect discrimination illegal in the above circumstances. Direct discrimination consists of treating a person less favourably on racial grounds than others would be in the same circumstances. For example, for a house-owner to refuse to sell his or her house to a person merely because that person is black would be discrimination.

Indirect discrimination consists of applying a requirement or condition which considerably disadvantages one racial group compared to another and which cannot be justified on non-racial grounds. For example, to require applicants for a labouring job to have a high standard of English would be discriminatory if it excluded members of a racial group which could do the job as well as others.

The 1976 Act also set up the Commission for Racial Equality (CRE), which was required to work towards the elimination of discrimination, promote equality of opportunity, and review the workings of the Act under review. The Commission was given the powers to assist plaintiffs under the Act, including providing them with legal assistance. 'Positive actions' provision were also included in the Act; that is, special provisions to help particular racial groups under-represented in given areas of employment.

On the surface, the 1976 Act might seem a comprehensive and potentially effective piece of legislation. It has almost certainly reduced the amount of open, public racism in Britain. It is also important as a major statement of principle in favour of racial equality (that is, equality of *opportunity* between the races). In practice, however, the Act has had very limited measurable effect. Only a few hundred cases of discrimination have been taken up by the Commission, and the majority of verdicts have gone against the plaintiffs. The concept of indirect discrimination has not been made practically applicable and so has been seldom used as a means of obtaining redress.

The 1976 Act is the major piece of legislation attempting to ensure equal opportunities in the liberal sense – that people will not be prevented from free and fair competition on grounds of 'race'. However, as the evidence cited in Chapters 4 and 5 shows, levels of discrimination in employment have been little affected (though direct discrimination has been reduced), and discrimination also continues in the areas of housing and education.

Two general responses to the limited effectiveness of the 1976 Act can be indicated. A range of liberal and radical opinions would like to see the Act strengthened and/or the introduction of new anti-racist measures. On the other hand, sections of the political Right have argued that anti-discrimination legislation has been ineffective and the CRE irrelevant: they would cut back or dismantle what they term 'the race relations industry' rather than strengthen it.

The CRE itself has proposed a number of changes to strengthen race relations policies, particularly at the level of implementation. These include clarification of the meaning of direct and indirect discrimination; setting up specialist tribunals to deal with discrimination with powers to enforce decisions; improvements in investigative procedure (to prevent delaying tactics); and a strengthening of sanctions against those illegally discriminating. The CRE also supports more effective positive action to redress the damaging effects of discrimination. Legal commentator Jeanne Gregory refers to the positive action provisions of the 1976 Act as 'a pale shadow' of comparable American provisions. There, for instance, both central and many local governments use *contract compliance* to increase the number of black employees (including those in higher-status jobs). This is done by making the granting of a contract to do work for the government dependent on meeting certain conditions in relation to the employment of black people (for example, employing a given target percentage by a given date). Another technique to increase levels of employment of black people in a given occupational area (such as a local police force) is to require that a certain *quota* of them be employed – perhaps subject to certain training requirements. Such policies are intended to compensate positively for previous racial disadvantage.

Positive action of this kind has never been a significant part of central government policy. Only one piece of legislation has positively 'discriminated' in favour of ethnic minorities in order to enable funds to be allocated specifically to them (Section 11 of the 1966 Local Government Act). To have discriminated in favour of black people would have been seen by leading politicians of both major parties as both a breach of the liberal principle of fair and equal competition and a confession that integration was not working. Section 11 was repealed in 1990.

In any case, during the Thatcher period of government, there was little if any chance of additional resources being allocated to the black community. As John Solomos puts it, a 'feature of recent political debates about race is that some of the most strident voices in contemporary political debate are raised not against racism but against "anti-racism"' (paper to British Sociological Association Conference, 1990). As we move into a period of political change and uncertainty in the 1990s, it is by no means clear what the thrust of government policy in the area of race/ethnic relations will be.

Racial harassment

Like racial discrimination in employment, housing and education, racial harassment is part of the everyday pattern of racism in Britain. It is perhaps the ugliest and most personally distressing aspect of racism.

The following cases of racial harassment occurred in Britain during the 1980s.

> As a boy sleeps, a pig's head, its eyes, ears and nostrils and mouth stuffed with lighted cigarettes, is hurled through the window of his bedroom.

A family do not leave their home after 7 in the evening; they stay in one large room, having barricaded their ground floor.

A family are held prisoner in their own flat by a security cage bolted to their front door by white neighbours.

A youth is slashed with a knife by an older white boy as he walks along a school corridor between classes.

A family is burned out and a pregnant woman and her three children killed.

(Examples cited in Paul Gordon, 'Citizenship for some: race and government policy, 1979–1989', Runnymede Trust, 1989)

A single incident of this kind would rightly provoke disgust and indignation in many readers, but from the wide perspective of the sociology of race relations the key question is how common racial harassment is in Britain. In turn, the answer to this question depends on how the term 'racial harassment' is defined.

Although many forms of racial harassment involve breaking the law, there is no single law making racial harassment illegal. In 1982, the London Metropolitan Police adopted a broad definition of a 'racial incident', which included all those 'which are alleged by any person to include an element of racial motivation, or which appear to the reporting officer to include such an element'. However, this led to the inclusion of many assaults or thefts of blacks against whites as racial incidents even though the racial motive in these incidents seemed slight or non-existent. It is more useful to regard a racial incident as one in which there is a specific racial motive, and on this basis surveys strongly suggest that the issue is mainly one of whites harassing blacks rather than vice versa.

A Home Office report of 1981 estimated that in any one year about 7,000 incidents would be reported to the police, but the Policy Studies Institute survey of 1982 argued that, largely due to non-reporting of incidents, the actual frequency of occurrence could be closer to 70,000. If the PSI estimate is even approximately correct, the answer to the question put earlier – 'How common is racial harassment in Britain?' – is that it is very common.

Of course, the amount of racial harassment varies from area to area. Roughly, the amount of racial harassment in an area varies in proportion to the number of black immigrants and their offspring resident there. Certain ethnic groups are also more likely to be victimised than others. Members of black ethnic minority groups are far more likely to be harassed than members of white minorities, but some reports, including one from a team at Brunel University, have found that the rate of victimisation among British Asians is twice as high as that among British Afro-Caribbeans. Both the Brunel survey – which covered several cities – and a survey by the Harris Research Centre, commissioned by Newham Borough Council in the East End of London, found that a quarter of British Asians reported being racially harassed in some way.

In response to the serious and extensive harassment described above, some groups in black communities, particularly British Asians, have organised in self-defence. This began in the mid 1960s, and by the late 1970s self-defence sometimes took the form of organised defence committees. For instance, in 1985, the Campaign Against Racism in Schools was formed in response to a rising tide of racial attacks against British Bangladeshi pupils in Tower Hamlets. Although the law permits self-defence, such groups risk their members becoming 'criminalised' themselves. However, the great majority of allegations of racial harassment do not lead to police prosecution, and many young Asians feel they have no alternative but to look after themselves.

Racial harassment, including physical violence, need to be put in the wider context of racism in Britain. There is nothing new in such attacks. An anti-Jewish riot in twelfth-century London resulted in 30 deaths. Still the object of racial hatred in London in the 1930s, some Jews formed self-defence groups against fascist threats. Blacks were the victims of racial attacks in several British cities as early as 1919. John Solomos suggests that the high incidence of racial attacks in the 1980s may partly reflect the fact that the National Front has turned away from mainstream politics to 'more direct' forms of action.

In his report on racial harassment for the Runnymede Trust (1989), Paul Gordon argues that the general political and economic climate in the 1980s has tended to be 'conducive' to racism in that immigration laws which can be seen as anti-black have been passed and few strong anti-racist statements have come from the government. As Gordon points out:

Every time the immigration rules have been tightened to restrict still further the entry of black people to Britain and every time there has been discussion about tighter immigration controls, there has been an upsurge in racial violence. In 1978, for instance, the year of Margaret Thatcher's 'swamping' statement (i.e., that she sympathised with those who feared being 'swamped' by people 'of a different culture') and the year in which the Conservative Party unveiled an even more restrictive immigration policy, there were no fewer than eight deaths from racial attacks.

(Gordon, 1989)

It seems, therefore, that more extreme racists take governmental concern about black immigration as a cue and excuse for violent racism. Perhaps leadership in the opposite direction – a sharp condemnation of racial violence – would have the opposite effect.

Crime and the Afro-Caribbean community: myth and reality

It seems highly possible that had the liberal reforms described in the second section of this chapter (pages 93–7) been more effective and discrimination against black people been correspondingly less, the rise in the crime rate among black youth and the tension and conflict between the police and the black community would not have occurred to the same degree.

Both official crime statistics and most scholarly studies tend to show a high rate of 'street crime' among Afro-Caribbeans, especially among the 15–24-years-old age group. There are various interpretations of why this is so, but the two extreme opposing positions are as follows:

1 Young inner-urban blacks actually *do* have a higher rate of street crime; and
2 Police activity (broadly, 'labelling' blacks as criminal) results in the difference from the general crime rate, although there is no real difference.

The police themselves tend to support the first position. For instance, the London Metropolitan Police have used victim surveys giving evidence on the colour of attackers as well as criminal statistics broken down by ethnicity to support their case that the rate of 'street crime' (for example, assault, robbery, drug-selling) among young blacks is particularly high. While many police accept that some racism exists in the force, racist labelling is seldom cited as a significant factor explaining black crime statistics.

Black sociologist Stuart Hall with his co-authors presents a complex analysis of black crime in *Policing the Crisis* (Macmillan, 1979), in which they see the oppressive role of the police as part of an oppressive society. They describe inner-urban areas with large, concentrated Afro-Caribbean populations as 'colonies' which respond to exploitation by developing their own alternative consciousness and way of life. Hall and his co-authors see crime or 'hustling' as part of this way of life or subculture. For many it offers more than a life of drifting between unemployment and dead-end jobs, with 'mainstream' opportunity closed by racism. Even so, it is only the most successful hustler who can avoid paid work altogether. Hall refers to the activities of these subcultures as '*cultural resistance*' because their members generally reject racial and economic exploitation. Reggae, Creole and rasta-style clothes are among the wider stylistic aspects of cultural resistance, some of which reflect the political-religious influence of Rastafarianism (see page 30).

Hall does not 'blame' the 'high' crime rate of black youth on police labelling. Rather, society's racism has 'marginalised' many young blacks and it falls to the police to deal with the resulting 'problem' of social control. As a result of these processes, a significant number of young blacks become 'criminalised'. Hall argues that in the early and mid seventies blacks were scapegoated as the cause, among other things, of white unemployment and of the 'rise in crime'. In particular, young blacks were often seen as potential 'muggers' – a perception certainly shared by numerous policemen, according to Hall.

Hall is careful *not* to equate 'cultural resistance' with political resistance. Writing more recently, Paul Gilroy gives more stress to the *potential* for cultural resistance to develop into political radicalism, but he, too, accepts that 'urban black cultures . . . are unlikely to be able to make the transition to more stable forms of politics' (*There Ain't No Black in the Union Jack*, Hutchinson, 1987). Perhaps the truth of this point was illustrated by the urban disorders of 1981 and 1985 when it never looked likely that economic and social grievance and discontent would translate into specifically political action.

Figure 7.4   **A subcultural approach to race and crime**
John Lea and Jock Young refer to the criminal activity of some young blacks and police racial stereotyping as a 'vicious circle' involving the following elements:

There has been a real rise in the types of crime in which young black people are disproportionately involved due to rising unemployment and its over-representation among young blacks due to racial discrimination.

In these circumstances, against the background of a high level of racial prejudice in British society, the police come to employ stereotypes of criminality among the black community as a whole and to employ saturation policing in such areas, the type of strategy which in the early eighties constituted the 'Swamp' operations in Brixton.

This leads to a progressive deterioration in relations between the police and all sections of the black community – despite the increased police resources being put into 'community relations' during the seventies – and results in a marked fall in the supply of information from the community to the police.

The result is that crime detection, because of less information and a rising rate of real crime, becomes increasingly harder and leads to a further incentive for the deployment of the SPG* in stop-and-search operations in an attempt to catch offenders.

* SPG – Special Patrol Group

(John Lea and Jock Young, *What is to be Done about Law and Order?*, Penguin, 1984, pp. 143–4)

John Solomos's observations on crime and the Afro–Caribbean community in *Race and Racism in Contemporary Britain* (Macmillan, 1989) are compatible with those of Hall. Solomos sees the way in which young blacks have been presented by much of the media and some agencies of social control as a 'problem' and even as 'the enemy within' (Solomos's phrase) as part of the racialisation of British public life in the 1970s and 1980s. They become blamed rather than the difficult social and economic conditions they and (in some respects) disadvantaged whites experience.

John Lea and Jock Young offer an alternative explanation of the role of black crime to what they term as the 'colonial' approach of Hall, Gilroy and others. They refer to this as a 'subcultural approach to race and crime'. They consider that young 'Afro-Caribbean people *are* more likely to be involved in certain types of crime *and* that police stereotyping also occurs. These two factors create a *vicious circle* which has the effect of worsening relations between the police and the black community – a major factor in several urban disorders. Their approach is outlined in more detail in Figure 7.4.

Conclusion

The relatively brief overview of racism, equality and the law given in this chapter affords scant basis for optimism. Despite the 1976 Act and the efforts of the CRE, racism remains commonplace in British life. Even a strengthening of the Act and the introduction of more positive measures to facilitate black achievement would, at best, only improve rather than radically change matters. However, Britain is far from a fascist country, though its culture is streaked with racism, some of a fascist character. Against this is a perhaps stronger tradition of liberal tolerance and, in addition, more recent radical anti-racism. The future of British race relations is poised uncomfortably between these various contending ideologies and forces with prediction on how matters will develop perhaps never less certain.

8 Politics and policy

Politics is about the struggle for power, and policy is about the purposes to which power is put. This chapter will draw on two approaches to understanding this struggle. First is the institutionalised area of political intercourse: central and local government, the political parties and pressure groups. For reasons given below, this area will be the main focus of this chapter. Second is politics – in this case, the politics of race relations, more widely conceived. It will be obvious from preceding chapters that the struggle by minority groups to achieve better access to and fairer distribution of resources encompasses employment, housing, welfare, education and other areas. Politics both affects and is affected by what happens in these areas. Similarly, the attempts by minority groups, particularly black people, to achieve positive identity (accepted by others as well as themselves), and the undermining of this by scapegoating and stereotyping, are partly a public and political process. Perceptions of black people as 'powerful' and 'beautiful' or as people 'from other cultures' by whom 'we' may be 'swamped' affect how black people are regarded and treated.

It is not easy to find an adequate way to draw the threads of the second approach together. In adopting a broader framework for analysing the politics of 'race', John Solomos suggests that in order to understand the changing content of racism and particularly its relationship to social structure, an historical approach is necessary. Solomos's own view is that during the post-war period British politics have been 'racialised' in that black people have regularly been presented in negative ways both through politics and the press. This tends to divide them from others, including many working-class people, with whom they have much in common in socio-economic terms. He argues that in the earlier post-war period, the fear of 'numbers' (of 'coloured' immigrants) was played upon, whereas, more recently, anxiety over the 'racial time-bomb within' has been the dominant theme. In Solomos's view, such images play the 'symbolic' role of focusing anti-black sentiment and action and detract from more constructive approaches.

The range of Solomos's approach is such that it cannot be adopted as the basis for organising this chapter, although his views, among others, will be a significant influence upon it. In any case, taken as a whole this book does contextualise British race relations in an historical and international context and examines interlinkages between the key areas of social life, including the economy and culture, in so far as they affect race relations. Necessarily, this has involved linking race/ethnicity with class, gender and age. How people 'see' these linkages and what they try to do about them is the stuff of politics.

The fact that this chapter is largely concerned with institutional politics is to complete the account of race relations given in the rest of the book rather than because a narrow view of politics is taken. In any case, the latter part of the chapter looks beyond conventional politics to consider 'cultural resistance', and the concluding section overviews the main ideologies and related strategies towards race relations in the light of the 'lessons' of recent history.

Three features which differentiate 'black politics' from those of the political 'mainstream' are worth pointing out. First, black politics have an intrinsic international aspect. Ties of blood and culture with their countries of origin and issues of common concern, such as apartheid and poverty in the Third World, give a global aspect to the political awareness of black people. Thus, when black politician Paul Boateng won Brent South for Labour in the 1987 general election, his apparently instinctive reaction was to say: 'Brent today, Soweto tomorrow.' Second, and self-evidently, the issue of racism is central to black politics. When racism has been effectively dealt with, black people will perhaps be free to 'be themselves', but that is far from the case yet. Third, black politics should be understood not only in conventional political terms but also in terms of the politically sensitised *life-styles* and cultures of certain black people, especially the young. Black literature and drama, and the life-style of members of certain movements, such as Rastafarians, often have a powerful, though sometimes indirect, political content. Just as Solomos suggests that the politics of racism should be broadly understood, so should black responses to racism.

National politics

Voting behaviour

A large majority of voters of both Asian and Afro-Caribbean origin vote Labour. Two main reasons can be given for this. First, the majority of British black people are working class, and as Labour is traditionally 'the party of the working class', it is perhaps 'natural' that they should tend to vote Labour. Second, black voters generally regard more favourably Labour immigration and race relations policies than those of the Conservatives. Table 8.1, opposite, is from a Harris Survey on what Asians and Afro-Caribbeans considered to be the most important issues in the 1983 general election. It is important to note that the order in which the issues are listed correspond to the Asian view of priorities, with the Afro-Caribbean given in brackets. Unemployment, which was very high in 1983, is overwhelmingly said to be the most important issue by both groups. This finding agrees with opinions expressed in sample polls of the whole electorate taken at this time. Significantly, the immigration/nationality issue is seen as the second most important issue by Asians but as only the fourth most important issue by Afro-Caribbeans. This reflects the greater difficulties now experienced in this area by Asians. It is worth noting that among younger Asians, immigration is receding in importance and is almost equalled by concern over education. Among Afro-Caribbeans education and the even more 'bread-and-butter' issue of the cost of living are seen as more important than immigration/nationality and, for the 18–24 age group, so are housing and police/law and order. Admittedly, some of these issues – such as police/law and order – have a strong ethnic-racial dimension, but, even allowing for the importance of immigration, black voters appear generally to have similar concerns as white voters: notably, employment, the cost of living and education.

Marxist commentators tend to argue that when other important social characteristics, such as class and inner urban residency, are considered, the effect of ethnicity on voting behaviour becomes 'negligible'. Given the above data on the importance with which immigration/nationality is viewed, this seems rather to overstate the case. There are several reasons why a black perspective or

Table 8.1 Political priorities of Asian and Afro-Caribbean voters (percentages)

The most important election issues*	Asians intending to vote (%)						Afro-Caribbeans intending to vote (%)					
	All	Con	Lab	Alliance	18–24	45+	All	Con	Lab	Alliance	18–24	45+
Unemployment (1)	71	39	79	72	70	73	67	57	72	56	72	67
Immigration/Nationality (4)	36	13	40	31	27	47	17	13	18	22	12	19
Cost of living (2)	19	34	16	19	17	11	27	30	28	39	34	30
Education (3)	17	26	14	19	23	10	23	30	21	28	28	13
Health Service (7)	13	12	13	19	11	13	13	17	14	—	9	18
Police/Law & order (5)	8	29	6	14	9	11	16	13	17	6	14	13
Housing (5)	9	5	8	17	11	9	16	17	15	22	16	15
Nucl. weapons/defence (8)	9	5	9	8	17	7	8	17	8	17	9	11
Taxation (9)	5	24	3	3	3	6	3	4	3	11	2	5
Trade unions (10)	4	5	3	—	3	4	2	—	3	—	—	5

* Listed by Asian ranking; Afro-Caribbean ranking in brackets
Source: Harris Survey for Black-on-Black/Eastern Eye Election Special, May 1983

perspectives are likely in British politics. From the point of view of most black immigrants, the Conservative record on immigration policy is worse than that of Labour even though Labour's record is seen as open to improvement. The 1981 Nationality Act passed under the Conservatives is regarded by many as frankly racist and accepted as such by both Labour and the Liberal Democrats. A further point is that the nature of black concern over major issues – such as unemployment and education – is likely to be substantially different from that of whites because of the effects of racism.

Black people in party politics at national levels

Black involvement in mainstream politics has been steadily increasing, as measured by both the number of blacks standing for representative office and the number actually being elected. In the 1979 general election, five black candidates stood for election for the main political parties. None was elected. In 1983, 18 unsuccessfully stood for election. In 1987 there were 27 black candidates, of whom four were successful. In 1987 Labour put up 14 black candidates, the Conservatives six, the SDP six and the Liberals one. All the successful candidates were Labour. They were: Bernie Grant (Tottenham); Diane Abbott (Hackney North); Paul Boateng (Brent South); and Keith Vaz (Leicester East). For there to be four black MPs is a big increase on none, but if blacks were represented in Parliament in the same proportion as in the population, the number would be close to 25.

To what extent is there evidence that the white electorate do not vote for black candidates simply because they are black? The answer to this question is vital. If equal opportunity does not occur in politics, then the outlook in other areas seems bleak. We can briefly examine three types of evidence on this issue: analysis of how black candidates fare in elections; historical precedent; and candidates' own impressions.

Data from election results are clearly the most convincing type of evidence. Marian Fitzgerald (see below) compared the results of the 18 black candidates of the 1983 election with their party's average for the same region; that is, how did they fare compared to white candidates in a similar context? The answer is that four fared better than their party's regional average, 13 fared worse, and in one case a comparison was not possible. In three of the cases where the result was worse than average, the difference was insignificant. Of the remaining 10, two did so badly that their results require particular attention and explanation.

Overall, Fitzgerald concludes that being black does not significantly disadvantage a candidate. The reason she gives for this is that people vote on party rather than racial lines. Interestingly, she finds support for this analysis in the case of the black Conservative candidate, Pramila Le Hunte, who fared the second worst of black candidates (and is one of the two cases referred to above). Fitzgerald argues that Le Hunte was an exception in that she was presented as a *black* Conservative rather than, as was the case with other candidates, a *party* candidate who happened to be black. As Fitzgerald puts it:

> It is only when they [voters] think they are being asked to vote for a candidate on the basis of colour, rather than party, that they set up a blacklash. To put it another way: white voters will sacrifice racial prejudice to party preference, but they will not vote for a candidate *because* they are black. Black voters are just as unwilling to vote on race alone, as the consistently poor results of independent 'ethnic minority' candidates shows.
>
> (Marian Fitzgerald, 'Are blacks an electoral liability?', *New Society*, 8 December 1983)

Arguably, the results analysed by Fitzgerald could be interpreted to indicate rather more racial bias than she suggests. However, as she points out, ultimately it is how black candidates will fare in *any* constitutency in Britain, whether or not it has a large black population, which will be the real test of racial bias in voting behaviour.

There are three precedents demonstrating the 'electability' of blacks to Parliament prior to the election of the four of 1987. The first, Dababhai Naoroji, was elected in 1892 for the Liberals, and the second, also of Indian origin, was elected as a Conservative in 1895. The third was first elected as a Labour and then as a Communist MP in the 1920s. Admittedly, these cases occurred some time ago, but alongside current examples they lend support to the view that black candidates are certainly electable in Britain – though to what extent remains to be tested.

Finally, at the level of individual impression, Paul Boateng found that his colour was not an issue in his successful campaign in Brent South in the 1987 election:

It's an issue that comes up in interview with the media, but it does not come up with ordinary people on the doorstep. Why should it? They are often already represented on the council [Brent South] by black people so it's nothing new to them.
    (*Guardian*, 2 June 1987, p. 8)

As Boateng implies, it may be the highly ethnically mixed nature of the Brent population that made colour such a non-issue there.

Black people in party politics at the local level

In a number of areas with large black populations, there has been an increase in the number of black councillors. In Brent in 1987, there were 20 black councillors (19 Labour, one Conservative). In the same year, there were three black council leaders in London, although within a year this was reduced to one. The resignation of two black council leaders, Linda Bellos in Lambeth, and Merle Amony in Brent, reflected the acutely difficult nature of inner urban politics especially in a period when central government funding cuts forced difficult decisions on local authorities with substantial social programmes.

Equal opportunity policies (see Figure 8.1) tend to be most vigorously pursued in local authorities with large black representation on their councils. For instance, Lambeth instituted detailed anti-racist and anti-sexist job recruitment procedures and in Brent a large team of teacher-advisers was set up to promote anti-racist education. Both councils fell foul of sections of the press but the development of equal opportunity and anti-racist policies is now more widely on the agenda.

Pressure groups and extra-parliamentary 'politics'

In addition to the directly party political activity described above, other black political involvement ranges from pressure group activities to the quasi-political utterances of poet-revolutionnaires.

Black pressure-group activity in Britain has never achieved the scale and effectiveness that it has in the United States – even allowing for the fact that blacks are a far larger proportion of

Figure 8.1 **A list of equal opportunity strategies employed by some Local Education Authorities during the 1970s and 1980s**

(a) collect statistics on the distribution and performance of ethnic minority pupils;

(b) disperse ethnic minority pupils (either by busing or adjusting catchment areas) if this does not contravene the Race Relations Acts (mainly before 1975);

(c) recruit staff to teach English as a second language and apply for section 11 funds to set up special provision for multicultural education;

(d) set up language and resource centres under the Urban Aid Programme;

(e) use the EEC social fund to set up mother-tongue teaching;

(f) investigate the composition of teaching and local authority staff and recruit and promote ethnic minority staff;

(g) appoint specialist advisers and inspectors for multicultural education and ESL teaching;

(h) give financial support and provide premises for ethnic minority community activities, such as supplementary schooling, religious classes and mother-tongue classes;

(i) liaise with and consult organisations from ethnic minority communities as well as local community relations councils (some financial support may be appropriate);

(j) help establish and fund curriculum initiatives and research projects;

(k) disseminate information and advice to schools by providing policy guidelines, objectives, examples of good practice and policy goals.

(E333, 'Policy-making in education', Module 4, p. 38)

the population there. One reason for this relative lack of impact is that many black activists have chosen to work through the Labour Party and, perhaps to a lesser extent, through the trade-union movement. Some have argued for the formation of a separate black section *within* the Labour Party on the grounds that Labour has failed to produce and deliver effective policies for black people. A section within the Labour Party is not just an informal group but has certain collective constitutional rights. There already exist youth and women's sections within the party. However, the party leadership is opposed to the formation of a black section unless full membership is open to whites as well as blacks, a position unacceptable to many who favour the formation of a black section.

The trade-union movement is also criticised as laggardly in the pursuit of the interests of black workers (though the formal statements of principle are impeccable) and slow to promote black officials. However, despite the existence of ethnic organisations, such as the Indian Workers Association, membership of the majority trade-union movement is actually somewhat higher among black minority employees than among whites.

A second reason for the relative weakness of independent black pressure-group activity may be that official institutions were set up in the 1960s quite soon after the arrival of the bulk of black immigrants in order to deal with racism and race relations. Currently, the Commission for Racial Equality and locally based Community Relations Councils provide a focus for black activism, which could be otherwise directed. However, much black political or, sometimes more accurately, politically tinged activity, such as Rastafarianism, simply bypasses official institutions.

From the 1960s until the end of the 1980s, responses to racial issues involving blacks were often organised on an immediate basis to meet a given issue or concern. A major concern of the early and mid seventies was the revival of the National Front and the growth of neo-fascism at street level. Paul Gilroy (1987) describes the anti-fascist responses, involving whites as well as blacks, as follows:

> Though the network of local groups developed and the need to combat the growth of Neo-fascist organisations was more widely accepted as the Nazi backgrounds of the UK leadership were gradually revealed, anti-fascist organizing remained locally-orientated and essentially small scale.

It was the formation of Rock Against Racism in 1976 by a small group of Marxists which both gave the grassroots anti-fascist

movement a stronger national dimension and shifted its philo-
sophy to broader anti-racist concern. This involved highlighting
the treatment of blacks by state agencies, especially the police,
courts and immigration authorities.

In the 1980s, the idea of using concerts and records or tapes as
a way of airing issues and raising money for a 'cause' was taken
up by more mainstream, liberal rock artistes. Black and 'Third
World' issues have figured prominently in this. The Bandaid concert promoted by Bob Geldof was spectacularly successful in
raising money for victims of the Ethiopian famine, and in 1988
the concert to celebrate the seventieth birthday of the then impris-
oned black South African politician, Nelson Mandela, dramatised
the issue of apartheid. In 1989, it was black sportspeople who took
a lead in condemning apartheid. Despite the international
Gleneagles agreement barring sporting links with South Africa, a
'rebel' English cricket tour of South Africa was announced in
August 1989. The party of 16 players contained two blacks.
Within a week both players resigned from the party reportedly
because of pressure from their own community. Among those
who powerfully articulated opposition to the tour was the black
sprinter John Regis.

Cultural resistance: urban disorder – 'real' politics?

Relatively low (though increasing) involvement in the formal
political system is insufficient outlet for the smouldering resentment among many blacks, especially younger ones, in urban areas
of a high concentration of black population. Anger or despair may
be caused by racism, poverty or unemployment.

The response of most black people to inequality and racism is
not primarily a political one – still less an extreme political one
such as adopting violent 'solutions'. The 'everyday' response to
inequality and racism occurs more at the level of culture and life-
style (see page 101) than in political activity. Many blacks are
culturally conservative and respectable (see page 84). However,
among a significant minority, particularly of younger blacks, the
response to unfairness and injustice is to 'opt out' or 'half opt out'
of 'the system' in favour of life-styles which enable them to express themselves better than they feel they can in the 'mainstream'.
In doing this, they may experience money and other practical

problems and risk conflicts with the law. Depending on the individual, the core of an alternative subcultural life-style may revolve around entertainment (he or she may become a musician or a sounds-system operator), religion (Rastafarian), or crime (pimp or illegal drug dealer). Sometimes, these strands inter-weave, but it is to misunderstand the nature of black youth subcultures to analyse them primarily in terms of crime (see page 84).

The simmering tension between some blacks – especially younger ones – and those they feel to be representatives of the 'system', such as teachers, social workers, probation officers and the police, often results in conflict. Twice in the 1980s, large-scale civil conflict occurred nationwide. A single incident – typically a clash between an individual or group of blacks and the police – can act as a catalyst to wider conflict and disorder. In many of the urban disorders of 1981 and 1985 incidents between young blacks and the police supplied 'the spark to the powder keg'. John Solomos argues that the reporting of these disorders and much political response to them tended to 'decontextualise' them from the complexities of racism and inequality and present them pri-marily as 'law and order' issues. This fostered negative popular images of black people and stimulated anxiety, if not panic, about them.

To what extent are the black youth subcultures political? Black Marxist writer Stuart Hall suggests that the term 'cultural resistance' better describes their attitudes and behaviour than 'political resistance' (1979). He would like to see members of these subcultures channel more of their energy and creativity into political activity. This would involve confronting and organising to deal not only with racism but also with the capitalist system which, he holds, generates economic and social inequality.

Weberian John Rex considers that members of black youth sub-cultures are more likely to be attracted to ethnic rather than socialist politics. Rex has for long argued that it is to be expected that various ethnic groups will organise to defend and promote their own interests at both the neighbourhood and wider levels. He contends that 'black power groups constitute for the immi-grants and the British blacks the functional equivalent of the working-class movement' (in R. Miles and A. Phizacklea, eds, *Racism and Political Action in Britain*, Routledge and Kegan Paul, 1979). From his own research with Sally Tomlinson in

Birmingham, he cites three types of black movements: orientated around a charismatic individual (such as the 1960s activist Michael X); ideologically orientated (such as the Muslim response to Salman Rushdie's *The Satanic Verses*); and issue-orientated (for example, the campaign against the 'sus' law which resulted in a very high arrest rate among black youth).

Perhaps it is less of a leap for young blacks to move in (and out) of ethnic politics of these types than into mainstream multi-racial politics. Ethnic concerns – in the form of defence of community members and territory against racist attacks – are the main motives behind both the Southall Youth Movement and the Bengali Youth Movement (Tower Hamlets). Rex is aware that, far from being socialist-inclined, black ethnic politics can seem quite reactionary to white observers. The behaviour of many Muslims in relation to the Rushdie conflict was widely perceived in this way (see pages 86–7) by white liberals and socialists although from their own point of view Muslims were responding to an extreme outrage against their beliefs.

'Race' and politics: the future

Setting aside the extremes of the National Front and black separatism, there is virtually universal agreement that black Britons are here to stay. Given this, the key issue is how they can be assured of the same rights and freedoms as other British citizens and, most would add, of a good quality of life. The other side of this issue is their impact on the rest of British life – which, finally, is a matter for negotiation, both publicly, through politics and policy, and privately, in everyday interaction.

As this and the previous chapter suggest, politics has a major role to play in the area of race relations, although precisely what this is varies with political perspective. Writing in 1987, and expressing the view of probably the large majority of contemporary politicians, liberal academic Michael Banton states:

> Immigration control has been achieved. There has been substantial progress towards integration, but this possibility is still not a reality for many people with African or Asian ancestry.
> (M. Banton, 'The beginning and the end of the racial issue in British politics', *Policy and Politics* 15(1) 1987, p. 47)

Such guarded optimism about progress so far is not shared either by John Rex or Marxist commentators. While the need to control immigration is recognised, the basis of British immigration and nationality legislation is seen as discriminatory by most critics of the Left. The 'other side of the equation', race relations legislation, is seen as still too weak and enforcement as often too difficult, lengthy and expensive. A number of local authorities now pursue positive action and anti-racist policies, and must have paid at least lip-service to equal opportunity policies for some time. However, socialists also consider that inequalities experienced by both blacks and whites require that they organise together to deal with them – an approach that leads towards 'class' rather than 'ethnic' politics.

The politics of culture have moved to centre stage since the late 1980s. Assimilationists make no secret of their wish to use public policy, particularly education, to inculcate 'British' values and tradition. The National Curriculum introduced by the Conservative Party is seen by some critics as ethnocentric and lacking the broader reference required by current global realities. As we have seen, liberal multiculturalists and radical anti-racists have their own views on what is a balanced educational diet. It is not clear that any of these preoccupations predominates among black people. Many Afro-Caribbeans seem primarily to want technically sound education, whereas among Muslims there is a distinct tendency to want to provide 'their own' education.

Given the plethora of problems and disagreements about policies, it is almost surprising that there has not been more conflict and violence in the area of race/ethnicity. It may just be that, despite acute differences and substantial injustice, the British people, black and white, do accept that coexistence means remaining in dialogue with each other and tolerating a great deal from each other. If so, eventually greater understanding and improvements in race/ethnic relations should occur; at which point, it should be possible to view variety and differences not as a threat but as a cause for celebration.

PART 3

Statistical data and documentary readings

9 Statistics

Introduction: the black and white numbers game

It is said that statistics can be used to prove anything. However, statistics are used to sustain not merely arguments but actions and policies as well. Indeed, the policies of governments are invariably supported by a battery of statistics, many of which are criticised by government opponents as either inaccurate or misleading. A classic debate of this kind in the 1980s occurred about the basis on which official unemployment statistics were constructed – which some argued were a gross underestimate.

Statistics on race and ethnicity probably provoke more heated debate than those on any other area. One reason for this is that certain race/ethnic statistics – such as those pertaining to crime – have been used, often imprecisely, to support negative stereotypes of black people. Another reason for concern is that race/ethnic statistics, particularly in relation to immigration, may be used to discriminate against a given group. Indeed, such is the concern generated that some have strongly argued that certain statistics about race and ethnicity should not be collected at all.

Ironically, some of the strongest arguments *for* the collection of race and ethnic statistics have come from those who want to ensure that blacks are *not* discriminated against and that they have equal opportunities with other groups in key areas of British life. Thus, local authorities and institutions which have wanted to develop equal opportunity policies have felt the need to monitor (including keeping statistics on) such matters as the numbers of black employees they have, their job status, and the number of black candidates called for interview (comparable statistics are kept about male and female employees or prospective employees in order to monitor possible sexist practice). Over a period, these statistics give an indication of how racist an institution might be and whether equal opportunities are available to blacks (and females) in practice as well as in law.

Reading 1

Many local authorities now include a section such as the one below in job application forms. Typically, they state that the information is solely to assist in the implementation of the local authority's equal opportunities policies and that it will be held in the strictest confidence.

		YES	NO
FEMALE			
MALE			
STATE IF REGISTERED DISABLED		YES	NO
WHITE	(UK	☐	☐
	(OTHER EUROPEAN	☐	☐
	(OTHER	....	
	(Please specify		
BLACK	(AFRICAN	☐	☐
	(CARIBBEAN	☐	☐
	(ASIAN	☐	☐
	(OTHER	....	
	(Please specify		

Questions

1 Explain the use of the term 'black' to describe people of 'African, Caribbean and Asian' ethnic background.

2 Give reasons for and against the use of the terms 'black' and 'white' in the information sought in the job application. Do you consider the information should be voluntary or compulsory?

Reading 2

In Chapter 3 it was suggested that the majority and ethnic minority cultures greatly overlap. This overlap is likely to increase as a growing proportion of members of black minorities are English-born. Already a majority of British West Indians are English-born (see chart (a) in Figure 9.1). The immigration of British citizens from the New Commonwealth and Pakistan was initially very rapid but has been slowing steadily since 1962 when the first Act aimed at achieving exactly this slow-down was passed. Because a

Figure 9.1

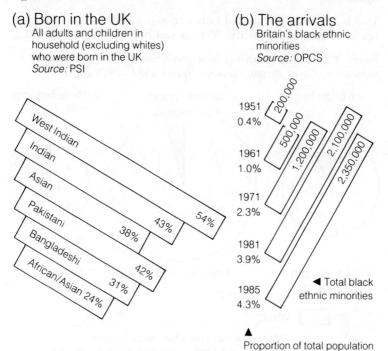

(a) Born in the UK
All adults and children in household (excluding whites) who were born in the UK
Source: PSI

West Indian
Indian
Asian
Pakistani   38%   43%   54%
Bangladeshi   42%
African/Asian   24%   31%

(b) The arrivals
Britain's black ethnic minorities
Source: OPCS

1951 0.4%   200,000
1961 1.0%   500,000   1,200,000   2,100,000
1971 2.3%
1981 3.9%   2,350,000
1985 4.3%

◀ Total black ethnic minorities

▲
Proportion of total population

Source: 'Database', *New Society*, 20 November 1987

relatively large proportion of the black immigrants tended to be of child-bearing age, black ethnic groups increased rapidly as a proportion of the total population (see chart (b) in Figure 9.2). However, the average age of blacks has now increased, so that the black minorities should settle at about 6 per cent of the total population around the year 2000.

Questions

1 Describe and explain changes in the rate of increase of black people between 1951 and 1985 as a percentage of the total UK population.
2 An increasing percentage of all black ethnic groups are born in the UK. Consider some implications of this in relation to *one* ethnic group.

Reading 3

This book has concentrated rather more on class and gender than age in relation to ethnicity. Yet, as can be seen from Figure 9.2,

Figure 9.2   Ethnic minorities as a proportion of each age group of the population, Great Britain, average: spring 1984, 1985 and 1986

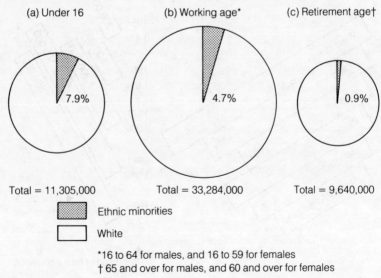

(a) Under 16   (b) Working age*   (c) Retirement age†

7.9%   4.7%   0.9%

Total = 11,305,000   Total = 33,284,000   Total = 9,640,000

▨ Ethnic minorities

☐ White

*16 to 64 for males, and 16 to 59 for females
† 65 and over for males, and 60 and over for females

Source: Labour Force Survey published in *Employment Gazette*, February 1991

the age structure of black ethnic minorities is worthy of remark. The questions probe the reasons for and consequences of this.

Questions

1 Why is the average age in black ethnic minorities so young?
2 How do you think the age structure of the black population might affect the perception of white people of the black minorities?

Reading 4

Table 9.1 compares the achievement levels of children from a number of ethnic groups at the end of the fifth form. It is taken from the Swann Report (1985). It is based on research in an outer London borough.

Table 9.1 Fifth-form examination performance by ethnicity and social class (percentages)

Examination performance	White (%)		Asian (%)		West Indian (%)		Other (%)		All (%)		Totals (%)
	MC	WC	MC	WC	MC	WC	MC	WC	MC	WC[a]	
High[b]	31	18	32	16	20	9	26	16	30	16	21
Medium	55	62	58	64	49	51	59	63	56	61	59
Low	14	20	10	21	31	41	16	21	14	23	20
Total (Number)	445	786	165	359	31	176	114	155	761	1,476	2,237

[a] MC = Middle Class, WC = Working Class. These categories are based on OPCS classification. See original paper for further details.
[b] High, Medium, Low. These categories are based on number of GCE 'O' level and/or CSE passes. See original paper for details.

Source: Craft and Craft (1983) in *Education for All* (The Swann Report), HMSO, 1985, p. 60

Questions

1 Compare the achievement levels of Asian and West Indian students. Explain the differences.
2 Briefly discuss policies that could be adopted to improve the performance of West Indian students.

Reading 5

Figure 9.3 gives some data on the membership of religious groups in Britain. The more vital groups are generally those of high membership, recent immigrants and their offspring.

Figure 9.3   Regional guide to religious revival (England and Wales)

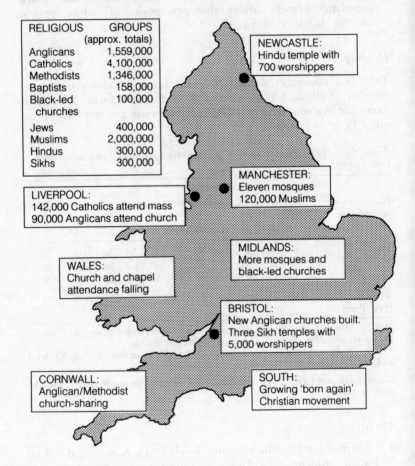

RELIGIOUS GROUPS (approx. totals)	
Anglicans	1,559,000
Catholics	4,100,000
Methodists	1,346,000
Baptists	158,000
Black-led churches	100,000
Jews	400,000
Muslims	2,000,000
Hindus	300,000
Sikhs	300,000

NEWCASTLE:
Hindu temple with 700 worshippers

MANCHESTER:
Eleven mosques
120,000 Muslims

LIVERPOOL:
142,000 Catholics attend mass
90,000 Anglicans attend church

MIDLANDS:
More mosques and black-led churches

WALES:
Church and chapel attendance falling

BRISTOL:
New Anglican churches built.
Three Sikh temples with 5,000 worshippers

CORNWALL:
Anglican/Methodist church-sharing

SOUTH:
Growing 'born again' Christian movement

Source: W. Schwartz, 'Evangelists lead revival of religion', *Guardian*, 14 July 1988

Questions

1 Write down one practice or belief you know about each of the Muslim, Hindu, Jewish, Sikh, Catholic and Anglican religions.
2 What benefits, if any, do you see as coming from knowing about other British religions than your own? Explain your answer.
3 With reference to Figure 9.3, account for the 'rise' of some religions in Britain and the 'decline' of others.

Reading 6

Statistically, blacks are more likely to be subject to agencies of social control than whites. Over twice as many young blacks as whites of school age are in schools for 'difficult' children; proportionately far more blacks than whites are in mental institutions (in some areas, perhaps 10 times more); and a much higher proportion of blacks than whites are in prison. Figure 9.4 illustrates the likelihood of going to prison by class, age and race/sex.

Figure 9.4   Likelihood of going to prison

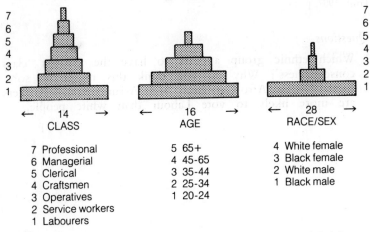

7 Professional	5 65+	4 White female
6 Managerial	4 45-65	3 Black female
5 Clerical	3 35-44	2 White male
4 Craftsmen	2 25-34	1 Black male
3 Operatives	1 20-24	
2 Service workers		
1 Labourers		

Source: John Lea and Jock Young, *What is to be Done about Law and Order?*, Penguin, 1984, p. 98

Question

1 Construct a 'stereotype' of the most typical prisoner. Give reasons why this type of person is the most likely to be in prison. (Note: This could be an essay-length question.)

Reading 7

Table 9.2 gives some data on ethnicity, class and voting behaviour.

Table 9.2 Class identity and voting behaviour of skilled, semi-skilled and unskilled manual workers (percentages)

	Afro-Caribbeans (%)	Asians (%)	Whites (%)
'Do you belong to a class?'			
All saying 'Yes'	70	57	79
'Which class do you belong to?'			
All saying 'working class/poor'	47	34	58
Voted Labour (1983)	65	68	43
Number	109	76	131

Source: M. Fitzgerald, *Black People and Party Politics in Britain*, The Runnymede Trust, 1987, p. 14

Questions

1 Which ethnic group appears to have the greatest 'class consciousness'? Why do you think this might be so?
2 Explain why Afro-Caribbean and Asian manual workers are more likely to vote Labour than white people.

10 Documentary readings

The purpose of this chapter, like that of the last, is twofold. First, it is to provide documentary support and illustration for some of the key points or perspectives presented in the main text of this book. Second is a related methodological purpose: this is simply to show by examples the importance of providing evidence for analysis and interpretation. The questions following each documentary extract focus on particular important points and on methodological issues and the relationship between the two. Each documentary reading links more or less closely with the statistical reading of the same number.

Reading 1 'Old' and 'new' racism – and the exploitation of labour

Chapter 2 describes how a major motive for allowing the influx of New Commonwealth immigrants in the 1950s and early 1960s was to ensure a supply of cheap labour. Here, A. Sivanandan gives a brief account of how, increasingly, labour from the Commonwealth is being replaced by even cheaper and more 'flexible' labour from the periphery of Europe and outside Europe. 'Third World' workers are 'cheap' not only because they can be paid low wages but because they do not have political or full social rights. A little belatedly (according to Sivanandan, due to slowness in technological innovation), Britain is joining the richer countries of Northern Europe in using international labour in this way. The concluding sentences of this quite difficult extract particularly repay close study: they analyse racism as a means of controlling migrant labour. Thus, racism is contextualised within Sivanandan's overall Marxist approach which – it will be obvious – is highly committed.

> A new racism is emerging from the interstices of the old. Less visible, more virulent, open to fascism and, above all, *European*, it is a racism directed against the migrants, refugees and

asylum-seekers displaced from their own countries by the depredations of international capital. Indeed, it is capital's need to break its national fetters and become European – to compete with American and Japanese capital – that has led to the growing influx of migrants into Europe. On the face of it, Europe does not want them: Third World immigrants create social and political problems. And yet it is their labour, cheap and captive, that fuels vast areas of an ever-expanding service sector (and makes their privatisation profitable). The problem, as before, is how to make economic gains without incurring social costs or political dislocation. And the answer, as before, is to let an unfettered racism – a racism open to market forces – exercise an informal control.

The development of such a pan-European racism is already present in Britain alongside the old British variety. But Britain, unlike the rest of Europe, has relied so much and so long on (imported) colonial labour and has been so slow to grasp the nettle of the technological revolution that the changeover to the European model has been slow and halting. Even so, the Immigration Act of 1971 had already heralded Britain's entry into Europe two years later by putting an end to all primary or settler immigration from the 'New Commonwealth' and opting, instead, for the *Gastarbeiter* system of imported labour. Commonwealth citizens were henceforth on a par with aliens. Other restrictions followed, making it virtually impossible for those already settled here to bring their fiancés and dependants over. . . .

The number of such immigrants might be higher in mainland Europe than in Britain, but here too the hotel and catering workers, the contract cleaners in hospitals, airports etc, the security guards in the private security firms, petrol pump attendants, domestics, fast-food assistants, hospital auxiliaries and porters and so many more – come increasingly from Colombia, Chile, Turkey, Sudan, Sri Lanka, Eritrea, Iran. And they enter not so much as migrant labour, tied to a work permit and hence to a specific job (such as the 14,000 Filipinos recruited in the 1970s into the hotel and catering industry and as domestic servants) but as refugees and asylum-seekers, fleeing the economic mayhem and political terror in their countries. With no rights of settlement, rarely the right to work, no right to housing or to medical care, and under the constant threat of deportation, the new migrants are forced to accept wages and conditions which no indigenous worker, black or white, would accept. They have no pension rights, no social security, the employers do not have to insure them – they are illicit, illegal, replaceable. . . .

The fascist dictatorships and the authoritarian democracies that western powers set up in Third World countries in their own economic and political interests are also those that provide the west with the flexible labour force it needs to run postindustrial society. Racism is the control mechanism that keeps that labour force within social and political bounds.

(A. Sivanandan, 'The new racism', *New Statesman and Society*, 4 November 1988, pp. 8–9)

Questions

1 Give reasons why British governments have cut back on immigration from the New Commonwealth and Pakistan (for example, in the 1971 Immigration Act).

2 Why is it that richer European countries have mixed attitudes to the 'freer' movement of international labour?

3 Given the difficulties they can experience, why do people from Third World countries seek to work in North-west Europe?

4 What is meant by the sentence 'Racism is the control mechanism that keeps the labour force within social and political bounds'? Do you agree with this analysis?

Reading 2 Class and race: a Marxist view

Chapters 1–3 present a number of perspectives on 'race' and 'racism'. In the following extract, Robert Miles gives a particularly 'pure' Marxist analysis of race. He considers that in capitalist society, race should be analysed in the context of class relations. What he refers to as 'racialised class fractions' are merely groups (fractions) belonging to the same class which have 'falsely' divided on the basis of race. He opposes such divisions among black and white members of the working class.

Consequently, I continue to argue that the 'race'/class dichotomy is a false construction. Alternatively, I suggest that the reproduction of class relations involves the determination of internal and external class boundaries by economic, political and ideological processes. One of the central political and ideological processes in contemporary capitalist societies is the process of racialisation but this cannot, in itself, over-ride the effects of the relations of production. Hence, the totality of 'black' people in Britain cannot be adequately analysed as a 'race' outside or in opposition to class relations. Rather, the process by which they are racialised, and react to that racialisation (both of which are political and ideological processes), always occurs in a particular historical and structural context, one in which the social relations of production provide the necessary and initial framework within which racism has its effects. The outcome may be the formation of racialised class fractions.

None of this denies that one response to racism may be the collective resistance of a proportion of those who are its object, but this resistance may include people who occupy different positions in production relations.

R. Miles, 'Marxism versus the sociology of race relations', *Ethnic and Racial Studies*, 7 February 1984, p. 219

Questions

1 Paraphrase or give a full précis of the above, admittedly difficult, passage from Miles.
2 Describe one view of race and racism that differs from that of Miles (see Chapter 4).

Reading 3   Black and white women in the labour market

Chapter 4 constantly stressed the links between race/ethnic stratification and class, gender and age stratification. The following is a succinct discussion of some key aspects of race/ethnic and gender stratification.

The position of black women in the labour market can be understood only by relating it to women more generally. I have dealt with aspects of this elsewhere and here wish only to take up one or two points highlighted in some recent discussions. Briefly the sexual division of labour segregates women into very few industrial sectors and within these they are usually in the lower segments of occupational hierarchies. They are in the main found in service industries, in jobs designated as semi-skilled, and they earn less than men. In the professions, they either constitute a very small percentage relative to men, for instance in law, medicine or university teaching, or where they are a higher percentage, such as in school-teaching, they are found disproportionately in the lower grades. As a consequence of this it has been argued that 'Black and migrant women are already so disadvantaged by their gender in employment that it is difficult to show the effects of ethnic discrimination for them'. But the same authors also maintain that 'black and white women may both be subordinate within a sexually differentiated labour market but black women will be subordinated to white women within this'. If we turn to the PSI findings, as the only existing representative national data, a number of points emerge. 'There is a much larger difference between white and black men than between white and black women in terms of job levels and in terms of earnings'. A suggested explanation of the similarity between the wages of black and white women which was reported in 1974, was 'that the enormous disparity between men and women . . . left little scope for racial disadvantage to have a further, additive effect'.

(Sheila Allen, 'Gender, race and class in the 1980s', in C. Husband, *Race in Britain*, Hutchinson, 1987)

Questions

1 According to Sheila Allen, 'The position of black women in the labour market can be understood only by relating it to women more generally.' Explain why this may be so.

2 Using evidence from elsewhere in this book, try to explain why females of Afro-Caribbean origin are especially likely to be of low social class status.

Reading 4   Warriors, Rasta heads and teachers

The formation of anti-school subcultures was cited in Chapter 5 as a factor contributing to the underachievement of some children of Afro-Caribbean origin. M. Mac an Ghaill examines the formation of several student subcultures of different ethnic origin in *Young, Gifted and Black*. A chapter, titled 'The Warriors: invisible form of resistance', examines an anti-school subculture of nine

English-born students of Asian origin. In the passages quoted, the 'Warriors' are questioned by Mac an Ghaill (MM) about relations between teachers and the 'Rasta Heads' (an anti-school, Afro-Caribbean group).

The Warriors suggested that the teacher racist stereotypes were not based upon any real differences in the behaviour of Asians and Afro-Caribbeans. Rather, it was the teachers' classification and labelling processes, to which both groups reacted, which determined teachers' perceptions of students.

MM: Do you think that West Indians cause more trouble than Asians?

Ashwin: No, don't be stupid, that's what teachers think. The Indians cause just as much trouble.

Raj: The West Indians are more obvious some'ow. They're seen more easily.

Iqbal: It's not, it's not that they cause more trouble. It's teachers, they pick on them more.

Raj: They treat them differently. I think they think the West Indians are dumber than us.

They challenged the teacher stereotype of the 'ignorant Afro-Caribbean' by pointing out that it was 'high-ability' Afro-Caribbean students who were involved in the anti-school groups:

MM: Do you think they are more dumber?

Raj: No I don't.

Iqbal: No, because they can do as well as Indian kids, better than a lot of them. The ones who have been in most trouble were the brainy ones, like Kevin and Michael, in the first year they were the brainy ones, really brainy.

These racially-based stereotypes acted as powerful social images and were of central significance to the teachers' perception of their interaction with students. They served to highlight the perceived 'rebelliousness' of Afro-Caribbean students and the perceived 'passivity' of Asians. The Warriors claimed that the Afro-Caribbeans did not cause more trouble for the school authorities, but that they were officially 'seen to'.

(M. Mac an Ghaill, *Young, Gifted and Black*, Open University Press, 1988, pp. 122–3)

Note: According to Mac an Ghaill's findings, more conformist, often middle-class students of Asian origin tended to perceive Afro-Caribbean students rather differently: in the words of one of them, 'The West Indians are always causing trouble.'

Questions

1 Try to explain the different stereotypes of Asian and Afro-Caribbean students held by some teachers.
2 What might the longer-term consequences of anti-school subcultural membership be?

Reading 5   Cultural conflict: freedom of expression and its limits

The debate and conflict over Salman Rushdie's book, *The Satanic Verses*, raised the frightening possibility of deep and irreconcilable division between two cultural traditions in Britain. On the one hand was the liberal tradition of 'free expression'; on the other was the refusal of Muslims to allow serious blasphemy against their religion to go unpunished. Here are two opposing statements on the issue.

Ian McEwan

I think it's important to bear in mind that if you live in a free society, one of the freedoms you have is to be daily outraged by what you read. I mean we are all outraged and sometimes even insulted by other people's opinions, and it's the very nature of a pluralistic society that we just learn to live with the scuffs and rubs of that kind of life. And the proper way to engage when you've been insulted is through the level of ideas. This book, however it's described – whether you regard it as an awful book, a boring or a brilliant book – is still only a book. It comes between no-one and their God. And it can only be properly engaged with at the level of ideas. That is the only way that we will learn, as atheists, Christians, or whatever, more about Islam – through that free exchange, not through book burnings and banning, which you should remember is murdering a book.

Shabbir Akhtar
Obviously what Ian is saying is true about the need for freedom. But of course, freedom of speech is not absolute in this country, or indeed in any country. I agree with you that in secular society one is outraged daily. But there are limits to that outrage, and there are certain things that we do censor. Certain kinds of racist material is not allowed and so on. But as far as the banning of this book is concerned, I think it is important, because I think otherwise the temper of militant wrathfulness which is essential to the preservation of religious traditions in secular society – especially a society which is aggressively secular – will be compromised.

(In conversation in *The Late Show* in L. Appignanesi and S. Maitland, *The Rushdie File*, The Fourth Estate 1989, pp. 228–9)

Questions

1 How free do you consider ethnic groups in Britain should be to pursue their own religion, education and cultures?
2 Suggest and explain the best solution you can think of to the Rushdie conflict.

Reading 6

This reading refers to some examples of the consistent concern of British governments about the numbers of non-white immigrants to Britain during the post-war period. The attempts to limit non-white immigration and the way the black community in Britain has been checked and monitored in relation to illegal immigration is one of the main examples to support the charge that British 'freedom' and 'liberalism' is sometimes – too often – 'only skin deep'. The concern of politicians and governments about how different ethnic groups 'get on together' is *in itself* not at all objectionable. The question is whether their statements and policies have helped or hindered the problem – or have even, in some cases, been racist themselves. For instance, may not Enoch Powell's 'prophecy' of violent racial conflict in his 'Rivers of Blood' speech have been partly self-fulfilling? You may find it useful to look again at Reading 1, which also bears on several of the themes raised here.

In the 1950s and early 1960s people from the Caribbean and Asia responded to the government's call by coming to this country in order to play a positive role in its re-building. Nevertheless, it soon became apparent that they were not necessarily welcomed, even in the worst jobs and in an inferior social position. The 1962, 1968 and 1971 Immigration Acts were used to restrict immigration to this country. In order to legitimize these controls over immigration, the collection of immigration statistics was used to monitor the operation of controls and to convince the white electorate that the government was doing its best to control the number of 'New Commonwealth' (that is black) migrants to Britain. By 1965 a strong cross-party consensus between the Conservative and Labour Parties emerged in favour of a dual strategy of immigration controls and measures to reduce the numbers of black immigrants and to integrate migrants already here into British society. In the now famous words of Roy Hattersley: 'Integration without control is impossible, but control without integration is indefensible.' . . .

From the mid-1960s the 'numbers game' became the focus of political propaganda. Enoch Powell's 1968 'Rivers of Blood' speech was but one example of the kind of images which politicians, the popular media, and the actively racist groups began to construct of Britain being taken over or destroyed from within by people from a different ethnic and cultural background. . . . Later, Conservative Home Secretary Reginald Maudling's message was that by reducing the number of immigrants one would enhance good race relations in this country and protect the dominant 'English' cultural values. This was a theme taken up by Margaret Thatcher in 1978 prior to the 1979 General Election in her famous 'swamping' statement, which took up similar themes to those articulated by Powell, among others, during the 1960s:

> People are really rather afraid that this country might be rather swamped by people with a different culture. . . . The British character has done so much for democracy, for law, and done so much throughout the world, that if there is any fear that it might be swamped, people are going to react and be rather hostile to those coming in. . . .

In the current context, the 'numbers game' is usually only associated with blacks. The now pending hand-over of Hong

Kong to China in 1997 and the potential 'influx' of Chinese who may wish to exercise their right to enter Britain may change this situation, and one should not at all be surprised if further legislation is introduced (as in the case of the Asians who were expelled from East Africa) to ensure that only a limited number of 'orientals' arrive in the UK. After all, during the late nineteenth century, fears about immigration centred on the numbers of Jewish and Chinese immigrants, and the restrictions on immigration introduced in the early twentieth century were largely aimed at these groups.

(B. Ashok *et al.*, *Britain's Black Population*, Gower, 1988, pp. 13–15)

Questions

1 Briefly describe *one* piece of legislation on *each* side of the 'dual strategy' referred to by Roy Hattersley.
2 Margaret Thatcher refers to 'the British character':
   (a) Do you agree with her description of it? Explain your answer.
   (b) Would you say that racism is part of 'the British character'? Explain your answer.

Reading 7   Positive discrimination

The following passage from the Scarman Report on the Brixton disorders of April 1981 provoked considerable discussion. In it, Scarman appears to come out in support of 'positive discrimination' in favour of blacks. However, it was apparent from later clarification (if not from the original statement itself) that Scarman favoured a 'mild' form of positive discrimination rather than the 'harder' form adopted by some institutions in the United States. He meant that more resources should be aimed at improving the economic situation and education of blacks, not that blacks should be favoured over those better qualified in a competitive situation. In the United States, some institutions recruit *quotas* of black students (and women), and some employers have adopted *targets* for the numbers of black employees they will have appointed by a given date (which may be taken to imply that a less well-qualified black may sometimes be appointed ahead of a better qualified white).

The attack on racial disadvantage must be more direct than it has been. It must be coordinated by central government, who with local authorities must ensure that the funds made available are directed to specific areas of racial disadvantage. I have in mind particularly education and employment. A policy of direct coordinated attack on racial disadvantage inevitably means that the ethnic minorities will enjoy for a time a positive discrimination in their favour. But it is a price worth paying if it accelerates the elimination of the unsettling factor of racial disadvantage from the social fabric of the United Kingdom.

(*The Scarman Report: the Brixton Disorders, 10–12 April 1981*, Penguin, 1982, p. 210)

Questions

1 Define the 'mild' and 'hard' versions of positive discrimination. Do you agree or disagree with either? Explain your answer.
2 What principles and policies, if any, has your own school or college adopted towards matters of race and ethnicity? How effective do you think they are?

Further reading

There is a wide range of material available covering race and ethnicity, but it is written for different levels and in varying styles. I stress below when a publication is likely to be suitable only for teachers or adult students. My own *New Introductory Reader in Sociology*, 2nd edition (Nelson, 1988) includes extracts from several of the publications listed here, including those of Castles and Kosack, Field, and Pryce.

A. Bhat, R. Carr-Hill, and S. Ohri, *Britain's Black Population*, 2nd edn, Gower, 1988.
In this book, the Radical Statistics Race Group looks critically at official statistics and related assumptions on race in several topic areas – well worth keeping for reference.

C. Brown, *Black and White Britain: the Third Policy Studies Institute Survey*, Heinemann, 1984: see S. Field.

Ellis Cashmore, *The Logic of Racism*, Allen & Unwin, 1987.
Cashmore has written widely and accessibly on race. Using ample quotations, this book explores the differing racisms of several social groups.

S. Castles and G. Kosack, *Immigrant Workers and Class Structure in Western Europe*, Oxford University Press, 1973.
This book remains a classic analysis, from a Marxist point of view, of post-war immigration from the New Commonwealth. Sivanandan's 'The New Racism', *New Statesman and Society*, November 1988, pp. 8–9, is a more recent piece in similar vein.

Centre for Contemporary Cultural Studies, *The Empire Strikes Back*, Hutchinson, 1982.
This is a seminal work on an area of increasing interest: race/ethnicity and culture. It is particularly useful on race/gender links. It is generally tough reading, though.

P. Cohen and H. Bains (eds), *Multi-racist Britain*, Macmillan, 1988.
This is a useful, if uneven, collection of essays and interviews on various theoretical, practical and policy aspects of race. Again, the material is quite demanding, particularly Cohen's interesting opening essay.

F. Dennis, *Behind the Front Lines*, Victor Gollancz, 1989.
  Black journalist Ferdinand Dennis brings an anecdotal touch to issues of race in this readable account of his impressions and experiences in a journey which takes him through several of Britain's main black population centres.

S. Field, 'Trends in racial inequality', *Social Studies Review* 1 (4), March 1966.
  This article has been of more use to me than anything else in providing students with accessible data on racism and racial equality in housing and employment. Field draws heavily on *The Third Policy Studies Institute Survey* (see C. Brown, above).

Charles Husband (ed.) *'Race' in Britain*, Hutchinson, 1987.
  This is probably the best general collection of reading covering race/ethnicity.

M. Mac an Ghaill, *Young, Gifted and Black*, Open University Press, 1988.
  This is an excellent account of British Afro-Caribbean and Asian pupil school subcultures – female and male. It is a useful source to illustrate interview technique.

R. Miles, *Racism*, Routledge, 1989.
  This is probably the most authoritative Marxist analysis of racism – but it makes no concessions to beginners.

Ken Pryce, *Endless Pressure*, Bristol Classical Press, 1986.
  First published in 1979, Pryce's participant observational account of black life-styles remains for me, despite arguable theoretical limitation, the best examination of the area.

J. Rex and D. Mason, *Theories of Race and Ethnic Relations*, Cambridge University Press, 1986.
  This is the 'theory' book in this list of suggested readings. It contains a number of important contributions, but for students Husband's edited collection is the more obvious choice.

J. Solomos, *Race and Racism in Contemporary Britain*, Macmillan, 1989.
  This is perhaps the best coverage of the politics of 'race'.

Index